IN HER OWN IMAGE

For K. R. M.

IN
HER OWN
IMAGE

ANNA MURDOCH

COLLINS
8 Grafton Street, London W1
1985

William Collins Sons & Co. Ltd
London · Glasgow · Sydney · Auckland
Toronto · Johannesburg

Permission to quote from the works of A. B. Paterson is gratefully received from Retusa Pty Ltd, Australia, and permission to quote from the works of Dame Mary Gilmore is gratefully received from Angus and Robertson Ltd, Australia.

BRITISH LIBRARY CATALOGUING IN PUBLICATION DATA

Murdoch, Anna
In her own image.
I. Title
823[F]   PR9619.3.M7/

ISBN 0 00 222768 1

First published 1985
Reprinted 1985
© Anna Murdoch 1985

Photoset in Linotron Sabon by
Rowland Phototypesetting Ltd
Bury St Edmunds, Suffolk
Made and printed in Great Britain by
William Collins Sons & Co. Ltd, Glasgow

ONE

It had been so hot that day in December, the day that Josie and her son arrived, that a fire had started in a bale of fermenting hay in the stable below BB's house. When she saw the green truck with the water tank on the back race over to the stable and her son-in-law, Harry, and one of the farm-hands begin furiously beating out the flames in the dry brown grass, BB had put on her gardening gloves and walked down quickly from Top House to help.

By the time she got there they had raked out as much of the hay as they could and were stamping on it with their feet and beating the stubborn flames as they spurted up now here, now there, with wet hessian bags. The farm dogs ran around barking, ugly blue mottled dogs, BB thought, and Jim, the farmhand kicked at them with his boots.

BB grabbed another sack, ran the water over it from the tank, and began beating at the grass with the men. The black ash puffed up around the edges of the sack as she hit the ground, as though it were a breathing thing they were attack-ing. Her efforts seemed so feeble, because the bag was so heavy, that BB began shuffling her feet on the little flames too, stamping on them at the perimeter of the fire. Jim looked at her with exasperation, his expression clearly telling her this was no place for a woman. It only made BB stamp more firmly. Harry moved the truck closer to the walls of the old stable, the green paint of the corrugated iron sidings blistered and peeling, and poured water from the hose as close as he could to the source of the fire. Rivulets of sweat ran down his blackened face. BB paused for a moment to wipe her own.

From out of the hay came a score of mice and Harry's setter, which had been quiet up till then, joined the other dogs in their furious excitement and pounced on a mouse with agility. The setter was just about to eat the mouse it had cornered between its paws when BB saw it and shouted, 'No, Ruby! No!' and the dog looked at her in surprise and then swallowed it anyway before slinking off to lie in the sparse shade of an oleander bush where it thought it could not be seen.

And then a curious thing happened, so odd, that BB later that afternoon could not get it out of her mind. She had just shouted at poor Ruby to drop the mouse when she had looked down at her own feet and saw, curled up at the toe of her right shoe, a small, burnt mouse, blackened with ash, singed almost beyond recognition, and she had stamped on it so viciously that she had felt its bones crush under her sole. It was a reflex action. She had looked up and saw that Jim was watching her, his eyes narrow under the brim of his stockman's hat.

''Fraid of a little mouse are you?' he drawled. He pulled his lips back and grinned at her. BB ignored him. Their dislike for each other was mutual.

The fire was under control and Harry said: 'You all right, BB? Want a lift up the hill?'

Harry whistled for Ruby as they got in the truck and the dog jumped into the cab between them, dripping saliva from its long pink tongue.

'I was a help wasn't I?' said BB slamming the truck door with satisfaction. Harry, used to his mother-in-law, merely grunted.

'What a mess,' said BB nonplussed, turning her attention to the holes in her stockings where sparks had melted her nylons. 'I'll have to change before they see me. Have they arrived?'

'No, not yet.' Harry reversed the truck and BB too turned her head to look over her shoulder. Jim was nonchalantly turning over the ashes making sure everything was out, 'Jim –' she began. But forgot immediately what she was going to say because Ruby began to burp and BB thought again about the mouse, live and whole in the dog's stomach, and wondered if Ruby was about to sick up fur and bones all over her skirt.

That afternoon, sitting on the verandah of her house waiting for her daughters to come, sewing up the hem of a dress, she could not stop thinking of how she had crushed the mouse without a moment's hesitation; had put her heel on it as though it were a serpent. Of course if it had been a snake she would have left it well alone and had Harry shoot it or break its back with his stockman's whip. She had seen him do that once when he was out riding with Liz, her elder daughter. It had not been long after Liz's and Harry's marriage. It was a brown snake, as deadly as its colour was plain, and it had gone across their path, right near the drive to their house, and Liz's horse had reared up and Harry had uncoiled the stock whip from the pommel of his saddle and cracked it only once and the snake, its back broken, lay quite dead. It had impressed BB at the time and she still saw Harry in this romantic role, dashing up on his horse to protect his woman. Pity it was the wrong woman. Liz was the most unromantic of women, a new breed, BB thought with a sigh. What a waste. Now if she had met Harry in another age, ah, that would have been different, or, if Josie and Harry had hit it off . . . BB bit the thread off her sewing and stuck the pin in the reel. Another ending, she thought.

BB was not by nature a morbid woman, but these days she was fascinated by endings. Even little endings, like mouse deaths. Which reminded her of something.

She rolled up her sewing and went inside the house and checked a mousetrap behind her refrigerator. It was still baited, waiting for the small visitor which kept nibbling at her electric wiring and shorting her out. Jim had been up twice to fix the wiring and had sneered at her and made such a mess, that she had sat out on the steps until he had finished, holding her broom and pan ready across her knees.

BB was not afraid of mice; not afraid of much (except perhaps Liz's temper, and *that* was something she tried to avoid); mice, she found interesting. She found them interesting because of what happened to them, not because of anything they did. Over the years she had collected stories of mice. Once, she had read about a perfectly respectable nanny who used to drop the mice she caught in the nursery into a bucket of water and hold them under with a fireplace shovel until they drowned. BB wasn't sure if she could come at that. She had a friend, too, while she was still living in England, who had the habit of dropping mice from the traps into her sink waste disposal and who would go on chatting over the sound of the mouse being ground up. That was in the days, of course, when larders were still being used, and refrigerators and sink waste disposals were just being introduced. That was in the days before BB had married Liz's and Josie's father and they had emigrated to Australia.

BB went back to her seat on the verandah, carrying a pot and a colander. Her seat was an old, unravelling rattan chair which she would not throw out. She was shelling peas for her dinner, popping the pods as she picked them from the colander on her lap and dropping the peas with a satisfying rattle into the pot on the floor beside her. She was thinking about mice, and about her marriages (what disasters *they* had been), and about death. All these endings occupied BB's mind so that at times she felt she was under siege from the ideas in her head. And into this maze, like an unwanted ball of string, unrolled the problem of how she could tell Liz her news;

which had nothing to do with any of these things. There was Liz's temper to take into consideration (Harry was the one who always soothed things between them), and a second consideration, no less important than the first, was that it was galling to BB's pride to ask her daughter for anything, knowing that she was really living here under sufferance to begin with. Like being in a grace and favour house. Just like the Queen let her relations stay in grace and favour places at Windsor Castle and Kensington Palace. But it made her mad to have to put Liz in that same category. She squeezed the pea pod she was holding so tightly that the peas shot out over the floor.

Liz was too independent and just too lucky. Why couldn't it have been Josie who married Harry? How cosy that would have been. She and Josie were alike. BB moved her chair awkwardly to fit into the shifting triangle of shade on her verandah. She was only sitting here to wait for the girls and she kept hoping the breeze that sometimes blew up from the Murrumbidgee in the afternoon would soon come.

And then she looked up and saw the girls walking up the hill. Girls she called them. Women really. She must have missed the car while she was cleaning herself up after the fire. She watched them toiling up towards her in the heat. Liz was wearing a hat and the brim kept flopping backwards and she kept ramming the crown more firmly on her head. They had ignored the road and were coming straight up through the grass, short and sunburnt and dusty, so that puffs of dust like small wings were at their heels.

BB was concentrating on her younger daughter, Josie, younger only by fifteen months, whom she had not seen since Liz's wedding twelve years before. Her hair was still the same. It looked thick and light brown and cut at the shoulder as it always had been. She swung her arms with the same old grace. It made her look very youthful, BB thought. She should have been a dancer, should have stuck to it. And in BB's

9

heart, in which, she acknowledged, there was little maternal instinct, there came a surge of interest, curiosity, or was it pride in this daughter who looked so like herself?

BB tried to identify her emotions as she stood up to watch their progress. In the same way she had been examining her feelings about treading on the mouse, murdering it, trying out different motives; was it deliberate, was it spontaneous, had she even thought about it at all? It was as though her emotions were contained in a thesaurus and she had only to pick out the right word for them to be explained.

So now, standing, cracking her knuckles nervously, she composed her face, first in one expression, then in another, trying out the roles she could play; how to greet this daughter whose life, quite frankly, she knew little about; a stranger to her, and yet a stranger who had come out of her own body; had been squeezed out, so that the muscles of her vagina, thirty-one years later, could still remember the sensation of that head passing through, like a hard, navel orange being forced through too small a tube. It never ceased to amaze BB. And it was thus with an expression of amazement on her face that she stepped off the verandah and into her garden to meet her daughters.

'She's got a beau,' said Liz, stopping for a minute, wiping her forehead and looking out from under her brim at her mother's house. Josie laughed.

'It's so long since I heard that word. In New York everyone has "dates". Makes me think of palm trees with men hanging from them in clusters.'

'If anything was hanging from a tree here it would be sheep.'

'Beaux. It takes me right back to our school days. Remember when there was a polio scare in Sydney and we were all choofed off to boarding school in the Blue Mountains?'

'Yes. She sent us back a day too soon.'

'She really couldn't afford it.'

'Beans. She had a new fox stole that year. Oh, do stand a minute Josie and let me catch my breath.'

Liz took her hat off and flapped at the flies which had settled on their backs. It was blazingly hot. They both turned, breathing heavily and perspiring freely, and looked back the way they had come. The Big House, Liz's and Harry's house, lay below them, massive and grey in its pale green jewel of a garden. The colour of an inferior emerald, Liz often thought, but loving it all the same.

The patch of green was an anomaly in the brown land-scape. When the river was high they could pump water out continuously to keep it green but with the trickle the Murrumbidgee had become this season, watering was done by hand when the sun went down. The river snaked lazily around the property creating a globular peninsula in which the houses and the stables, the yards and the shearing sheds, were scattered with no apparent design. The trees in the bend of the river shimmered silver in the stillness and beyond the trees, the hills of the Murrumbidgee country lay gently and endlessly blue.

'I'd forgotten how beautiful Tiddalik is,' Josie said stretch-ing her arms out and splaying her fingers as though to touch the river and the sky.

'It's a ridiculous name,' said Liz. 'Did you know it meant Big Frog? Tiddalik. Cynthia told me. It's from an aboriginal tale about a frog that drank up all the water from the river and creeks and caused a tremendous drought.'

'How apt,' said Josie.

'Yes. Cynthia would tell you aboriginal myths all day long if you let her — and then nothing gets done in the house. I suppose it must have looked exactly like this when the first settlers came, dry, waterless.'

'But it does rain sometimes?'

'Oh yes. Even the story tells us that. When Tiddalik drank

up all the water, the other animals decided that if they could make the frog laugh, it would spit out all the water it had swallowed, and the creeks and billabongs would fill up again. So they tried everything to make the frog laugh, but without success until an eel began to dance and the frog did laugh then. He laughed so much that his mouth burst open, the water poured out and the drought was over.'

Josie moved her foot for a firmer stance on the steep slope and a myriad of grasshoppers flew crackling down the hill in a chain reaction.

'Who's mother seeing?' she asked.

'Mr Doughty, the chemist from town.'

'Mr Doughty? Is he still alive? He must be seventy at least.'

'Seventy-two. And he adores her. Can't imagine why. They go to Mass together on Sundays. My God, wait till you hear her on religion. She's making up for lost years. And I tell you she's getting more difficult to deal with every day.'

'Well it's probably her age.'

'Menopause you mean? She's been going through that phase then since the day I was born!'

A fly landed on the corner of Josie's mouth and she spat it out with distaste. Her sister laughed and Josie allowed herself a rueful grin.

'You never get used to them, no matter how long you live here,' Liz said flapping her hat between them. 'Come on, I can see BB waiting for us.' They started climbing again and the cloud of flies settled once more on their backs.

'You're thin,' BB said accusingly, looking at her younger daughter perched on the arm of the sofa. They had moved inside because the sun was too hot on the verandah. The room was dark and stuffy, the curtains and blinds, even the door closed against the heat. An electric fan standing on a cloth-covered sewing machine protestingly pushed the hot air in the room around and around. Above the hum of the fan you could hear the twittering of BB's pet bird in the kitchen. Liz sipped at a cool glass of lemonade that BB had brought in, carefully removing a bird feather from the rim before she drank. BB caught her doing so.

'No need to be so fussy, Liz.' Liz sighed and settled back to watch her mother and Josie renew their acquaintance. How alike they looked. Even more so, now that Josie was older. They were both smaller and neater than herself. She had always felt like the big cuckoo in the nest. BB and Josie had the same round brown eyes, though BB's had always had a look of ambiguity about them. They never did reflect what she really thought and consequently her mouth and her eyes always seemed to be in conflict with each other. Josie's eyes were the same as she remembered from when they were little girls; still soft and, – vulnerable. Liz thought with an inward sigh what a luxury that must be to keep.

'You're thin,' BB repeated, 'and you sound . . . American.' She looked at Josie as though she had come from another planet.

'Wait till you hear young Alex,' Liz said.

'I never thought you'd sound like them.' BB shook her head with disapproval. Liz sucked loudly on her drink, forcing herself to refrain from mentioning the fact of BB's own quite clear British accent.

'Alex didn't come up to see you because he's exhausted, poor kid,' said Josie. 'He fell asleep as soon as he got to his room.'

Liz was watching her mother in the dim light. She could not imagine what was making her fidget so, even worse than usual. Her hands kept straying across the tray on the table, moving the jug an inch and tracing the wet circle endlessly with her fingers.

But Liz couldn't read her mother's mind, though sometimes she thought she came damn close, and Josie went on talking about New York and how bad the weather had been when they flew out of Idlewild Airport and how she and Alex had nearly missed the plane because President Kennedy had been in New York that day and the traffic had come to a standstill. Liz said she would give anything to be sitting stark naked in a deep drift of snow right at this very minute.

BB said: 'It's so long since you lived in Australia Josie, you've forgotten how hot it is.'

'New York gets hot too,' said Josie, 'but then, you've never come.'

'Oh, it's such a long way away,' said BB, her voice reflecting the geographic isolation she felt. 'Everything is such a long way away from here.' She glanced at Liz.

Liz merely grunted and lay further back on the sofa with her eyes closed. She felt like a deflated balloon; there was no air and she wished BB would get to the point of whatever it was that was bothering her. BB's fingers were twisting a ring of three narrow bands of stones she wore on her left hand (one for each husband, Liz would say maliciously).

'It will be nice for us to be a real family at Christmas, for once, won't it Liz?' BB said. 'So nice for me to have my family together for the first time; me and you and Josie and my grandchild and Harry. And in fact when you told me that Josie and Alex were coming over, it got me thinking.'

Liz's eyes opened a fraction and through their slits she stared at the ceiling waiting for her mother to continue. A fly was buzzing incessantly around the anodized light fitting. Liz waited for it to land.

'And it being Christmas and the time for renewal and forgiveness and so on . . .' BB's eyes turned to Josie, 'Your Jews after all have their days of atonement, don't they? All I have is my piddling confessions, dribbling out bits for Father to hear.' Her brown eyes turned again to Liz, 'So I thought it was time I made atonement too: once and for all. So I wrote and asked *my* mother if she would like to join us too.'

The fly kept buzzing around the room. BB waved her hands in the air as though to ward off flies and interruptions.

'Now I know it costs a lot of money to fly here from England. But it's not going to cost me a penny. Daphne's got her own money and she's paid for the fare herself. Now isn't that something? Here I was thinking all these years that she had no . . .'

Liz interrupted, 'How long is she staying?'

'Well that's the other thing, dear.' BB took a deep breath and plunged on, 'I've asked her to come and live with me – for good.'

The information dropped into the room like a stone into a deep well. There was no sound at all. The fly had landed.

When at last the stone reached the bottom, Liz said, 'Oh hell, Mother.' (BB noticed that Liz always called her Mother when she was angry.) 'What on earth's got into you? She's an old lady. She's very happy and comfortable in England. Her friends are there: she knows no-one here. You're not even close. Oh, Christ.'

'Liz, you don't know. You should read her letters. She's so lonely poor thing. And the cold hurts her leg. Ever since she was hit by a truck last year on a zebra crossing. They put a pin in her hip you know,' she said in an aside to Josie. Josie was biting her lip. She looked to Liz as though she wished she had stayed in New York.

'Her hip worries her terribly,' BB went on, her voice beginning to quaver. 'There she sits in her two-up, two-down house, in that miserable village in Essex where it's always raining. Always raining. And mice.' BB's voice strengthened. 'Mice in her house. It's too wet for them outside. The time when I went to visit her I went to use the toilet, and do you know what was floating in it? A mouse. A dead mouse. It gave me quite a turn.'

'Too wet inside for it too, from the sound of it,' said Josie. Liz was too angry to laugh.

'Anyway, here I was with this house,' BB swallowed, 'thanks to you, Liz, and Harry, with a spare room and a little garden and all the sunshine the world has to offer.' She plucked at her skirt with her right hand. 'And it took me so long to find her. You have no idea what I went through. It wasn't so easy in those days to find out your real parents if you were adopted. Perhaps now I can do all the things for her I was never able to do before.'

Liz could not contain herself any longer.

'BB, you were not the slightest bit interested in her after you met her in England. Not the slightest. I know why you've brought her here. You found out she's got some money . . .'

'That's a lie!'

'. . . and then she seemed much more interesting.'

BB's mouth quivered like a child.

With an angry jerk Liz picked her hat up from the floor where it had fallen and stood up.

'Then, I don't know what's got into your head to bring a seventy-year-old woman . . .'

'Sixty-nine,' said BB.

'. . . a sixty-nine-year-old woman, out to a strange continent on the other side of the world. The heat'll probably kill her if she does make it. And what are you going to do with her out here? Spend your days together crocheting? It's ridiculous!'

'Couldn't she just come for a visit instead?' said Josie.

'Too late,' said BB, her voice expressing both despair and triumph. 'She's already on her way, you see.' She took a flimsy blue airmail letter from her pocket and smoothed it on her thigh before handing it to Liz. 'She's arriving tomorrow in Canberra. I thought Jim, or someone, might drive in and pick her up . . .' Her voice trailed away waiting for Liz's reaction. 'She won't be any trouble.'

Liz was furious at being so manipulated. Again. It was always the same with BB; she rushed into things before she had thought them through and then expected others to help her get out of trouble.

And BB could still so easily put her on the defensive, as though Liz were in the wrong, and BB was just a sweet, thoughtful daughter trying to look after an aged parent.

'You might at least have discussed it with me,' said Liz, knowing how weak that sounded. She crossed to the front door and opened it as if she needed air and stood leaning against the jamb looking out, with her arms folded. Behind her she heard her mother get up and the two women go into the kitchen with the tea things. She was by no means unfamiliar with her mother's capricious ways, in fact Liz had lived with them so long and suffered under them too, that you would have thought she was immune from attack by now. Yet her mother was able still to set something fluttering and jumping inside her as easily as she had when Liz was a child.

There was the time when BB had taken up the saxophone and would practise at all hours so that the girls could hardly sleep. Even a note from Mother Superior at the Mercy Convent enquiring what was wrong in the household that the girls were falling asleep at their desks, had no effect. It was only the fading of BB's fantasy, together with the difficulty of the instrument, that finally brought an end to it. What these mundane problems had done, however, was teach Liz how to cope. She became the little mother at a very young age. It was she who took Josie to her dancing lessons in the Palings Building in Wynyard on Saturday mornings. She who tied her sister's plaits and rubbed the spots off her blazer with a damp cloth before school. She who made the sandwiches. And once, when Josie had toothache and BB would not take her to the dentist because she was flirting with the idea of becoming a Christian Scientist, Liz took Josie and had the rotten molar pulled out in one visit after school.

Liz put her hand on the jamb of the door and looked out

over Tiddalik Station. A small fleck of paint fell off under her hand. The house needed painting but not this year. The fencing had to be done first. There was a section near the main road where the sheep kept getting through. And they hadn't been able to put down any superphosphate for years. The land was starved for it and she longed to improve it, as Harry did. But there was never enough money. At best, this land which Harry and she loved, was marginal. The rainfall was always too low, or too late, and the rocky outcrops of limestone, ridging the paddocks like ribs, made little arable farming sense. At worst, in years of drought, as now, they lived on an overdraft from the local Commonwealth Bank. And BB had thought she was marrying money. A queer little smile slipped over Liz's lips as she looked at the brown hills basking like a sleeping dog in the late afternoon sun. She was aware of her mother's thoughts about Harry.

'Are you coming, Josie?' she asked over her shoulder.

Josie and BB came to the door. Liz held open the flyscreen and they went onto the verandah.

'I still have some Christmas shopping to do,' she said, 'so I suppose I could do it tomorrow and we could pick up Daphne at the same time.'

'Oh, I knew you could work something out,' said BB clapping her hands with delight and coming to the steps with them. How BB's too evident relief irritated her elder daughter.

'I'm only going to pick her up, BB,' said Liz. 'It's your decision to bring her here and it's your problem.' She felt like Pontius Pilate as she went down the steps. The sun licked them like a flame as they came out of the shade.

'It's so hot,' said Josie, easing her damp shirt from her back. 'Do you mind if I go for a swim?'

'Of course not. There's still a pool deep enough in the bend down below the house. In front of Bull Paddock. Do you want me to come?'

'No. No, I really would love the walk and a bit of cooling off. I'll sleep better tonight.'

BB was on the steps with them and having sorted out her immediate problems was looking around for another. And as always she found one.

'Oh, just look at my geraniums! Really Liz, it's that cat of yours, he comes up here and eats them. Eats the leaves off them. Oh, it really is too much.'

'Don't blame the cat, BB, it's probably the 'possums,' said Liz. 'And anyway the cat would get rid of the mice you keep complaining about . . .'

'A cat would eat my budgie.'

'. . . instead of bothering Jim all the time.'

'I certainly don't like having Jim hanging around here all the time.'

'Yes, we've noticed.'

But BB wasn't listening. She was already poking at the soil of her potted geraniums with a stick and breaking off the nibbled leaves with her fingers. Liz looked at Josie and raised her eyebrows. They shared an unspoken thought. Silly old bitch. And in the sharing of that thought about their mother, Liz realized it was as close as she and Josie ever had been. And it made her sad to realize that it was the first time since Josie had arrived that they had really looked into each other's eyes. It embarrassed Liz and it must have embarrassed Josie, for they both dropped their gaze.

'Goodbye, BB,' said Josie. But there was no reply. The sisters set off with an awkward half-wave to each other. One towards the river, and the other towards the house; each towards what beckoned them most on Tiddalik.

· TWO ·

Liz was glad to get out of her mother's house; to breathe in the clean dryness of the air, no secrets tainting it; to see around her the hills unfolding one behind the other, nothing she did not know hidden in their gullies.

She knew what was there, without seeing it; knew, but could not distinguish from this distance, the miles of unpainted wood and wire fences stretching across the paddocks, around the hills and gate-legging at rivers and old boundaries. Just as she knew, but tried to ignore the rows of boxes in the dimness of BB's room. She knew they were there; knew too there were others just like them, but more haphazardly arranged in toppled order, in the closets, under the table in the kitchen, on the verandah and in the crawl space of the house. And without looking, Liz could describe what was in them: the sheets of recipes and clippings from past issues of the Australian *Women's Weekly*; household hints BB would never follow; meals she would never cook. There were yellowed pages from the *Daily Telegraph* with articles on gardening and advice to the lovelorn; plants she would never grow and advice she had never followed. Like her mother's dreams, they remained as tantalizing fragments of ideas; hopes, once embarked upon but never brought into harbour.

Under the pedal sewing machine, not much used these days, more boxes were stacked. This one filled with half-finished sweaters and lengths of cloth; three and a half yards of blue and green brocade bought at a sale at Foy's in Sydney, 'it would make a lovely cocktail dress, Liz, if only I had the time to run it up'; that one full of lengths of gingham and cotton, and cut-off pieces from brittle and fragile paper patterns, stuck with rusted pins, all jumbled in a pillowcase because 'they might come in handy one day'. There were boxes and spools of thread, balls of wool, extracted zippers from skirts and clothes long disposed of. And in the boxes, other boxes, shoe boxes of buttons, hooks and eyes, saggy elastic wound around cards, crocheted squares of wool in harsh colours that only needed, said BB 'to be tacked together and it will make a lovely rug, or a shawl, or a baby's blanket. You never can tell when you might need it.'

These things, not often seen, but always present, depressed Liz so much that she avoided going up to BB's house as much as she could. She refused to eat there because the kitchen was just as bad, except there, instead of clippings, the boxes contained utensils and crockery, mostly broken or unusable, and some never unwrapped from their newspaper from the time BB had moved in God knows what was in the bottom of some of those boxes; tomato sauce bottles growing fungi, Liz thought with a shudder; or old carrots that had perhaps rooted through the damp cardboard bottoms, through the linoleum, into the earth below the house. It made her sick to think about it.

But it was not just the dirt of her mother's house, not just the squalor of it that depressed Liz; but the untidiness of it all. The untidiness of BB's life. The boxes represented to Liz all her mother's failures. Liz thought about it as she walked down the hill, the sun beating down on the back of her neck even through the straw of her hat. She thought about BB's inability to follow a thing through, to complete anything she ever started. (And the few things she did pursue always ended in disaster.) How could BB live with all those reminders of false starts and broken promises? So much unfulfilled. There were times when Liz would look up at the house from the safety of her own and see it as a ship on the high seas of the brown land, sailing forever under full canvas, and always going in circles.

The house was the source of the grievance between BB and Jim. Stupid old Jim, Liz thought, who had little time for him herself. But Jim had originally lived in Top House, had done so since Harry's father died, and when BB came to live at Tiddalik (and did Liz regret nothing more than opening her mouth about that), Top House, being the closest house to Liz and Harry on the property, and the second best to boot, was given to BB. Jim hadn't really complained; he was too fond of Harry, whom he'd doted on since he was a boy. He had moved without fuss into a shearer's cottage on the high land, two miles up the cutting. But he was hurt and would show his resentment in many little ways and would make snide remarks, referring to BB as 'that fuckin' barmaid', but not when Liz was within earshot.

And BB had done nothing to ease the transition, and had, on finding any of Jim's belongings still in the house, placed them out in the open, halfway down her drive, 'for all the world to see!' spluttered Jim (as though any living thing besides the family and the animals traversed this road); but Jim would be livid with proud, icy rage at the sight of an old ashtray with a flip-top chrome lid on a stand, or a faded picture of prize-winning heifers cut from the local newspaper and stuck in a cracked, black plastic frame, and once, a badly chipped porcelain night-chamber, with native wild flowers hand painted on the sides, stood for hours on the drive until Jim came past and swept it with hurried tenderness and ill-concealed rage under his shirt and stalked proudly down the hill to the truck.

Liz had found it amusing at first as she watched Jim's clobber move out and BB's move in. But the situation never got any better and simmered along with many petty occurrences and 'no speaks' on both sides, only to erupt in bitter accusations at certain times when the crust of their animosity burst.

Liz came to the bottom of the hill and headed for the stable block. She wondered if Harry had finished work yet or if he were in the farm office. He spent more time there it seemed than out in the paddocks these days. Playing scientist, she called it. Harry had long since given up trying to explain to Liz the results of his sheep breeding experiments. He had been at it a long time. But they disagreed on how the farm should be run; Liz wanted a quick turn over; after all it was she who had to pay the tradesmen, but Harry dreamt of long-term improvement. He wanted to breed a better sheep, that was all. The drought they were now going through hadn't helped either of them.

The stable block at Tiddalik was a handsome, low-slung building of grey limestone blocks, hand hewn, so that the angles and the planes left by the adze showed the red clay of the soil they came from. Liz's approach from her mother's house brought her past the killing yards first, where the sheep, which they used for their own table, were brought for slaughter. This afternoon, three small sheep lay bleating in the heat, watched by the cattle dogs, howling as usual where they were chained in the shade under the water tank.

'Oh, shut up,' Liz said, heaving a small stone in the dogs' direction. They put their black snouts on their blue-spotted paws for a moment until she was safely past, then started their howling again as soon as she was gone.

Liz came to the office and pushed open the heavy red-painted door and adjusted her eyes to the dimness after the glare outside. Harry's pride and joy. An office made it sound much grander than it was. It had once been used as a store-room for grain and the air still seemed thick with the fine smell of it. It had one small window high on the wall in which a pane of glass was missing. An old, cream-coloured refrigerator, its cord disappearing through the missing pane, stood in the corner humming noisily. There was a single electric bulb with a string attached hanging from the ceiling. The walls had been whitewashed a year ago and a black and white aerial photograph of Tiddalik with the paddocks marked on it in red ink, hung crookedly from a nail. Liz straightened the picture with one finger. There was a battered, once varnished, desk and a chair; the desk neatly covered with stacks of veterinary supplies (the 'fridge contained more of the same), some yellow Manila folders and pamphlets on sheep breeding and cattle diseases; some books on the same subjects; a microscope; a lamp (with its cord dangling); an oblong blue box of glass slides; some pencils; some pens, nibbed and ballpoint; a ruler in a jar, and a bottle of Quink ink (blue-black). Liz picked up a pamphlet and flicked through it. God, how did Harry read all this stuff? Liz moved the ruler an inch. Over the desk was a calendar, sent by the local stock agent each year, with a highly coloured picture of red Scottish cattle eating lush green grass. Each year's calendar was indistinguishable from the previous one. Beside it, suspended from another nail, its pages fluttering in the faint breeze from the open door, hung Harry's sheep breeding charts.

Although Liz was heartily tired of Harry's talk of sheep (she had been listening to the same stuff for twelve years), she liked this room: because of its order: everything in its place. It was in this way, she supposed, in their hankering for order, that she and Harry were most alike, though for Harry she suspected this liking was innate, and for herself it was something she had learnt and acquired.

Liz, who liked order, who had imposed it on herself, stood and surveyed the room and she felt, just by standing there, that she was holding everything together. For a moment she had the ridiculous sensation that if she moved everything would fall apart. So she stood very still in Harry's most private room and listened to the sounds of the farm; the dogs, the bleating sheep, the cry of cattle, the hum of the 'fridge and the generators. They were good sounds for Liz, solid evidence that all was well in her world; everything in its place, nothing to surprise her.

In her own house – the antithesis of BB's – it was the same. In her kitchen even the spice racks were alphabetically arranged. Cynthia, who helped her in the house, said she just would never get the hang of it, and anyway why couldn't the cinnamon go next to the paprika? And the towels in the linen closet, now there was another thing. Liz liked them folded her own particular way and graded them in colour and size. It made not the slightest difference to Cynthia who kept on shoving them in in her own way and it gave Liz a perverse pleasure to find them in a jumble because she then had the excuse periodically of pulling them all out onto the floor. And Liz could then sort them, pulling the bindings straight because they kept shrinking, putting the points of the corners together and then stacking them, colour by colour, so that their rounded folds faced out like rows of corrugated towelling and it was a pleasure to look at them. Sometimes, walking along the upstairs hall and passing the linen closet (making sure first that Cynthia wasn't around, for the girl after all was only eighteen and Liz didn't want to hurt her feelings), she would open the door just to see the towels so neatly arranged, until gradually, over the next week, Cynthia would manage to 'get it back to normal' with a sigh of relief.

The sound of the truck roaring into the yard and the impatient toot of its horn brought Liz back to the present. She pulled the door closed behind her and went into the sun. Harry was at the wheel of the truck, the cattle dogs he had taken with him, and Ruby, perched on the flat-bed behind him. The dogs under the water tank were barking at their mates. Harry's face under his wide brimmed hat looked worried.

'Is Jim here?' he shouted above the noise.

'No,' she said walking towards him, 'I haven't seen him. What's up?'

'His mare's running loose up the drive. He went out on Peg just after lunch. We had a fire in the old stables so we split up to get through the rest of the work.' As he was speaking, Peg, Jim's mare, came trotting into the yard, her reins hanging in front of her, making her lift her feet higher than usual. Harry switched off the truck, swore at the dogs to shut up, and got out. Liz was already advancing on the horse, its ears back, her voice low and soothing.

'Whoa there, Peg. Whoa there.' They grabbed the reins and Peg was immediately docile. A quick check with their hands on the horse showed nothing broken and Harry led it into the stable where they slipped off her bridle and saddle and Liz gave the horse a wipe with the saddle cloth.

'He said there was a calf with a cancerous eye up in Osage Orange Paddock,' Harry was saying, standing characteristically with his legs apart and his hands on his hips. He eased his back for a moment with a small wince and she noticed it, as she noticed everything about him, but said nothing.

'Old bugger might have been thrown. I'd better go and look for him.'

'I'll come with you,' said Liz. 'Josie's gone for a swim and Alex is sound asleep.'

They got into the truck and Harry started the engine.

'How are they?' he asked.

'They're fine.'

A pause.

'Alex is a lovely boy. He looks just like Josie. Same brown hair. Same eyes.'

A longer silence fell between them; their own lack of children a gnawing contention. They drove towards the main road, the metal of the window frame burning Liz's arm as she leant against it.

'Has BB seen them yet?'

'She's seen Josie. But BB wanted to see me. God, Harry, you've no idea what she's gone and done. She's asked her mother to come here! To live!'

They were out on the main road now heading for Osage Orange.

'I thought her mother was dead?'

'She is, her Italian mother. This is Daphne she's talking about. Her real mother. The one she finally found in England. You remember when she went to England the first year we were married? She'd just divorced the undertaker, and she put an ad in the paper and one of her cousins got in touch.'

Harry laughed. He had a strong laugh and put his head back when he did. Liz watched his Adam's apple.

'That could only happen to BB,' he said. He shook his head in disbelief. But nothing his mother-in-law did ever surprised him. He'd once come across her in a sudden rain squall sitting in her driveway with her hair plastered flat to her skull. 'What are you doing?' he had shouted at her from under the dryness of his riding slicker. 'It's lovely,' she had shouted, 'Come and see!' But there was nothing to see but mud and puddles. Liz said the only reason he could cope with BB's eccentricities with such equanimity was because she hadn't got at him yet. But she would. Oh she would, and then who'd be laughing?

'It's not funny,' said Liz. 'I'm mad as hell. She had no right to do it. And you know who will be the ones to clear up the mess afterwards – you and me. She'll be sick of that old lady inside a week, I'm telling you.'

'Well, you don't know that for sure.'

Harry stopped the truck and got out to open a gate. Liz slipped into the driver's seat and drove over the cattle ramp. Once they had not needed to have a gate at the ramp but people were coming out from Canberra now with pick-up trucks and Tiddalik had lost one or two steers. Harry had found the chopped off legs of a young steer up here some months back and the gate had been put in.

When Harry was behind the wheel again Liz went on:

'If there's one thing I do know Harry, it's my mother, and I wouldn't rely on her to wake me up for breakfast.'

They had come to Osage Orange Paddock, named after the grove of trees on its western boundary which dropped its green, inedible fruit constantly on the ground. They both saw Jim at the same time, sitting under one of the trees, propped against the trunk with an empty bottle beside him.

'Why, he's drunk,' said Liz tightening her lips, 'again.'

Harry drove over towards the trees.

'Poor old bugger,' he said.

They stopped the truck and got out. Liz stood with her arms folded looking down at Jim. Her voice was angry.

'Harry, you'll have to get rid of him if he keeps doing this. He's useless to you.'

'None of us are perfect, Liz,' he said leaning over and picking up the older man effortlessly in his arms.

'You'll hurt your back,' she said. He ignored her.

'Come on, you old bastard, let me help you on the truck.'

The affection in his voice only irritated Liz further.

'Oh, it's hopeless talking to you. Hopeless. He's just using you. No-one else would give him a job!'

'That's what I reckon,' said Harry.

Liz bit back a retort with difficulty. It infuriated her when Harry was so damn patronizing, particularly when they both knew he was right. He would seldom argue with her, and because he didn't, she always felt he had won. She watched Harry lift Jim onto the back of the truck, tucking him in between the pile of hessian bags as though he were a baby. The dogs were licking Jim's face.

'Get off, Ruby,' said Harry.

'Are you listening to me?' Liz was still standing with her arms folded.

28

'Well, I'm trying not to, love,' he said. He gave her a grin. It made her feel even more impotent, that she could not goad him into anger, could not vent her frustrations on him. With a suppressed oath she jumped into the cab and slammed the door and sat fuming while Harry eased himself behind the wheel, patted her leg, and started the engine.

In the kitchen of the Big House (no-one knew where these names came from, they just always had been known as Big House and Top House), Cynthia, her wide black brow creased in concentration, was peeling potatoes. She was thinking about her wedding dress when she heard the sound of the truck and the beep of the horn at the back door. She was thinking that if she eased the tucks out, she could still get into the dress. The horn beeped again. Curses on all men, she thought as she slipped carefully off the kitchen stool and padded across the kitchen floor.

'Give us a hand, Cyn?' shouted Harry from the back drive.

Cynthia banged out the flyscreen door, adjusting her weight carefully in front of her. She was due in January and it was the hottest December she could remember. It had taken her this long to get old Jim to agree to marry her. If he didn't bolt in the meantime, she thought. She ought to hobble him like a bloody horse she ought.

'He's tied on a beauty this time, Cyn,' said Harry as she came around to the back of the truck where Jim was lying happily and totally drunk between the bundles of hessian and the empty water tank. He smiled stupidly at her as the dogs licked his face and wagged their tails.

'Oh, Jim,' she said, 'What have you done?' Her deep brown eyes reflected the resignation in her voice. It was as if she could already see her future and it held no surprises. Jim began to sing and hiccup:

> I bought a run a while ago
> On Country rough and ridgy,

He lost the words somewhere and hummed.

> Dee da dee da, dee da dee da . . .
> The Upper Murrumbidgee.
> The grass is rather scant, it's true.
> But da dee da dee dum . . .
> The sheep can see a lovely view
> By climbing up the ranges.

'Old Banjo's not going to help you now, Jim,' said Harry climbing onto the flat-bed to get at him.

Jim grabbed his arm as Harry tried to lift him.

'It's true, isn't it? I'm never going to have a place of my own, right? This is it, isn't it? R – ruddy r – ridges of the Murrumbidgee.' He stuttered over the words and hiccupped. There was a cut over his left eyebrow and the blood had dried and caked over his eyelid.

'This is your home, you drunken old bastard,' said Harry slipping his arms under Jim's armpits and hoisting him to the edge of the flat-bed. Jim had gone a total dead weight. The women struggled to help him off the truck. Jim grabbed at Cynthia.

'Give us a kiss, Cyn.'

'We'll put him in the back room till he sobers up,' said Liz.

This was a seldom used room containing an old broken divan and little else. It led off the net-enclosed verandah that ran the length of the back of the house. Liz and Harry got him off the truck and struggled with him to the door. Cynthia, propping him up, sometimes with her arms, sometimes with her belly, lurched along with them. She pulled open the door and they got past her awkwardly onto the verandah. The smell of rosemaried mutton from the kitchen wafted over them. It reminded Jim of another song and he began humming away under his breath.   ·

Cynthia opened the door of the small room, moved a couple of crates out of the way and part of a milk churn that had never been fixed, and stood aside while Liz and Harry rolled Jim onto the faded brown divan.

'Christ, he's really gone to Gowing's this time,' said Cynthia starting to take off his boots. 'Where'd you find him?'

'Up in Osage Orange, happy as a sand boy,' said Harry taking off his hat and wiping his brow.

'He's goin' to end up just like my Dad,' said Cynthia with a shake of her head. She looked up at Harry for a moment and her eyes filled with tears. 'Just like my old man. What a shame.' She pulled off his boots and a stream of blood spilled out on the floor. 'He's so damn drunk he doesn't know where he's hurting.'

Liz went out of the room and along the verandah to the kitchen for a bowl of water and some disinfectant. In the small room Harry squeezed Cynthia's shoulder.

'He'll be all right, Cyn. Clean him up and let him sleep it off.' He went to the door.

'Mr Barton?'

Harry stopped and turned around.

'Thanks.'

He nodded and went out.

Jim opened one eye.

'Give us a kiss, Cyn, while they're all gone.' Cynthia was leaning over him unbuttoning his shirt.

'Come on, Cyn.'

'You're drunk as a piss-pot,' she said but her eyes were roughly tender. He was old enough to be her father, but he was kind to her. He had never hit her, never asked for anything she hadn't wanted to give. He had never been mean to her like some of the nuns at the Home, who used to be so nice to her black face when the priests and the monsignors were around, but used to pull her hair and twist her ear lobes when she couldn't understand her schoolwork. Only some of them, but they were the ones you usually remembered.

He grabbed one of her hands and held it tightly.

'You smell of soap and potatoes. Good, clean smells. Give us a kiss, darl'.' He arched his head up and rubbed his chin against her breasts, hanging large with childbearing above him.

'Don't be daft,' she laughed, 'not now.' But she let him nuzzle at her for the briefest moment and imagined how it would be to have her own baby's mouth on her, and then she moved away as Liz came in with a white enamel bowl and the first aid box under her arm.

'Thanks Mrs Barton,' she said taking the bowl from Liz. She glanced at Jim. He had fallen asleep.

'Gee, I'm sorry,' she said. She knelt down again beside the divan.

'It can't keep on like this Cynthia, you know,' said Liz watching Cynthia bathe the cut on his forehead and then turn to the cut on his foot. 'We're short handed enough as it is. There's only Jim and Reilley on the place now. Harry has to rely on Jim.'

'Oh, yes, I know. But don't you worry Mrs Barton. You've been real good to me, with the baby coming and all. Jim'll be OK. Really. He's just a bit upset these days. You know, with me and the baby and the wedding. He's managed to escape a woman so long I guess it's all a bit of a shock to him. They can't cope, can they? Men I mean. He just needs me to straighten him out, that's all. And you know he'll do anything for Mr Barton. Anything. He'd sell his soul for him, if he had to.'

Cynthia snipped the bandage and cut one end in two long strips, knotting it and winding it around Jim's foot. Her long black fingers made the bandage seem very white.

'Just wait till we're married. He'll change. It'll steady him, I promise.' She got heavily to her feet, picked up the bowl of bloody, milky water and followed Liz quietly out the door.

Liz left Cynthia in the kitchen and went to find Harry. He was in the downstairs bathroom splashing water over his face and hands. She was going to tell him what a fool he was to keep Jim on. Jim was increasingly nothing but trouble. And what was she going to do about her mother, for God's sake, and Daphne? And with Josie and Alex here now and Cynthia so pregnant she could hardly bend over, it all gave her a headache. But instead of berating him, she put her arms around him and stood for a moment resting her head against his back. She was not by nature a demonstrative woman and she felt, under Harry's damp shirt, the muscles of his back stiffen, and he stopped with the lather on his hands, only for the briefest moment, but they both registered the hesitation. He smelled of sweat. Today, with her mounting tension, the effect on her of her family's proximity, she found the earthiness of it reassuring. The rank smell did not bother her, so for once she did not say, for heaven's sake go and have a shower before we eat. It did not bother her.

What did disturb her, and it disturbed her more than she cared to admit, was to see Cynthia's innocent love for Jim. That old sod. But it had reminded her of how she once used to feel about Harry. She too had once had that same euphoric emotion, an unshakable belief in her ability to change him. And at first she hadn't even thought he needed that. She stared at the crisscross threads of his Oxford shirt. She had once thought of Harry as a god, oh that was too strong a word, but certainly she had once thought of him as being high mettled and pure; had felt that she could look into every crevice of his character and find him blemishless. Like herself? How things changed. No matter how she tried to trick herself by ordering the parameters of her world, things did change, had changed, but she could not work out if that was because of Harry or because of herself?

Sometimes she wondered, listening to him splash, keeping

her arms around him, if he felt it too. That, whatever they had shared was evaporating, but, like old perfume, traces of the scent still lingered. Had they just grown too used to each other over the years? But in familiarity there was comfort. Was that love? Was that what happened to it? She had never seen either familiarity or comfort in BB or her father, certainly not when they were together. There were times when Liz thought there might only be so much love to go around and she had had her turn, she and Harry, and now it was Cynthia's turn; Cynthia swelling with love's physical evidence. Liz thought suddenly of Harry's breeding charts fluttering in the wind. Her own barrenness engulfed her.

'What's the matter?' he asked reaching for a towel.

'Oh, nothing,' she said taking her arms from him and standing seeing her own reflection in the bathroom mirror. How pale she looked beneath her sun-browned skin; how empty she felt; like one of those dried shells of the Christmas beetles hanging outside on the trunks of the eucalyptus. Such pretty bronze-green husks. Harry had once told her they were the colour of her eyes. In the old days that was of course. Such pretty husks, but brittle, threatening to break. She thought of them as ancient talismans and sometimes at night when they would sit outside after dinner, she would pick them off the papery barks of the trees and place them in a circle on the neck of her sweater or shawl, like a necklace of old-fashioned garnets.

She stood in the high-ceilinged, cool bathroom on the black and white tiles and watched her husband comb his hair. She watched him pat the back of his head self-consciously where the thick light brown hair was growing imperceptibly thinner. His blue shirt stretched across his shoulder blades. She wanted to touch him but her arms remained limp at her side.

He was vain. She wanted to prick him.

'Is all this primping for my benefit?'

He hung up the towel and faced her.

'What do you think?'

He smiled at her, did not touch her, circled her to get to the door. He was too damn good-looking.

'Harry,' she said, 'did you know that the Roman gladiators were only five feet tall?'

He laughed out loud and opened the door.

'And do you know that you are getting more like BB every day?'

· THREE ·

Josie had walked the long way down to the river, thankful to be out of her mother's house and into the vast emptiness of the paddocks and hills. The sky was so high, deep and featureless, like a snowfield back home, that Josie wished she could leave her footprint on it. She picked up a branch of yellow-box gum crushing the leaves and inhaling the smell of the eucalyptus deeply. It was like a refreshing gust of liberty after the stuffiness of BB's house; and BB's mind. Josie had not wanted, on the very first day of her visit, to become enmeshed in BB's web and had felt, coming back to visit the family for Christmas, that her own adult strength would be enough to avoid it. Now she was not so sure.

She threw the leaves away and swishing the branch set off down the paddock towards the river. She could see the Murrumbidgee gleaming like a cool promise through the trees.

Beautiful river. It reminded her of Sydney Harbour, how it had gleamed up at her through the plane window that morning, glancing painfully off the silver wings. Hello old friend it said. How you've changed. You haven't, she had thought looking down, pointing out the sights to Alex. Her hometown. The water always gleamed here. Even on grey days it had seemed to her like steel, never losing its shimmer. She remembered so vividly how the water of the Harbour had shone just this way when she was a little girl. 1942.

The light from the water bounced through the trees then. They had a rented apartment at McMahon's Point, she and Liz and BB. Money was short and BB had turned to her dressmaking skills to make ends meet. It was a confused time. Things changing. Things breaking up. The war was on; Sydney was on blackout alerts. The Grace Brothers building and the Marcus Clark building had both been taken over for military and government use. Even the girls' bodies were changing. Liz and Josie had bought their first box of sanitary towels together and BB, full of her own sensuality but unable to acknowledge theirs, had thrust a booklet on *What is Menstruation?* at Liz and that completed their sex education.

Josie was going through a religious phase that year and had developed a crush on one of the nuns at school and spent much of the time wandering around the McMahon's Point apartment with a black cardigan buttoned around her face and a white handkerchief tucked across her forehead. 'Do I look like a nun?' she would ask Liz, as she caught sight of herself in the mirror. Liz would glance up from a book; 'You look sick'; dismissing her with a crushing finality before sweeping her eyes back to her book.

It was the year their father left. He was too old for the war and his civilian job as a fitter and turner was finished. Industry was turning to munitions and he told them he would have to go to Melbourne where he could get work in a factory. He told them this on the morning he was leaving. 'Look after your mother till I get back.' They were in the kitchen and he was formally dressed in his only suit, a striped brown wool with wide notched lapels, and he was sitting with BB on his knee, BB in a pink padded housegown, his hand, the permanent grime of oil under the fingernails, resting on the satin. The girls were embarrassed at this unusual sign of affection. And then he was gone. Josie began to suspect then that love meant you hurt people, a puzzling lesson that BB, through her behaviour, continued to reinforce.

Not long after he had gone, BB decided that she could not go on sewing dresses for customers who never paid on time. So she left the dresses, some finished, most not, hanging on their hangers from the doors and walls of the living room and hall, and went out and got a job. As a barmaid at the local pub, The Prince of Wales on Blues Point Road. Allied troops arrived in large numbers that January and the city was bustling and rowdy. BB went so far as to dye her hair blonde. 'You're only born once,' she said. She began to speak of Blue Orchids and Menzies Mannequins, and said, 'Wouldn't it rock you?' after every sentence and called every gadget, a 'doovah'. It was at the pub, while on duty, that she met the journalist.

She brought him home once or twice and they would sit kissing in the living room. Once Josie couldn't stand it any longer and put on her black cardigan and handkerchief and marched into the living room, brushing past the ghost dresses with missing arms and hanging hems and said, 'Excuse me. I've just come to get my missal.' BB just told her not to be so silly but after that she didn't bring him home any more. Or anyone. At least not while they were there.

Instead, she just stayed out later and later. The girls would creep into their bed, they had always slept together in a double bed, holding each other and listening to the waves lapping at the bottom of the street. Each time a ferry came in, the waves would lap and slap louder. One or two cars would come and go, their headlights dim because of the brown paper masking them, but sometimes a faint beam would cross the bedroom wall. And then, bliss. They would hear her key in the lock and see her shadow flit over their bed through the open door. 'Is that you, Mummy?' 'Hush. Go to sleep.' And they would turn and snuggle into each other and allow themselves to sink into that sleep where they knew they were safe, safe, safe; that she was there, only a thin wall away, thin as a membrane, and she would come in if they called out, her nightgown, silky as her shadow, brushing against them as she leaned over. If they were very lucky, and she was feeling particularly kind, she would get into bed between them, and they would curl into each other. Josie would hold her mother, feeling against her own small body the forbidden softness of her breasts and stomach under the silkiness; smelling the feminine smell of her, sometimes musky, sometimes sweet; the oil smell of her hair, the hint of tobacco smoke caught in it; the dryness of her breath that reminded Josie of cloves.

But one night she did not come home. They had curled up in their bed together, Liz and Josie, but they were still afraid for the darkness that night seemed extra bleak and the street lights were all out. They could hear the lap of the water against the Harbour wall at the end of the street. It made Josie think that she was on an island that was gradually being eaten away by the sea. Liz had got up and gone to their mother's room and got out their father's great army coat, of khaki-coloured wool, which he had worn doing his military service before they were born. Liz had put it over them and they had fallen asleep at last, though Josie woke once in fright when the buttons on the epaulets tangled in her hair.

In the morning, BB was still not there and Liz dressed Josie and herself, and braided Josie's hair and made their sandwiches for lunch. In the afternoon when they came home there was a telegram slipped under the door. They read it while they made strawberry jam sandwiches. The bread under its wax wrapping was hot from the sun where it had been delivered on the doorstep. 'NOT COMING HOME STOP CALL DAD COLLECT MELBOURNE 28718 LOVE MUM.'

And so BB went off chasing her own rainbow and their father came back. They stayed on at McMahon's Point and he found a job as a janitor looking after a boiler in a school. He hated the job. He was a gentle man but he could not overcome his setbacks. To be cuckolded by a journalist and

God knew who else, and finally to be almost unemployable, eroded any self-respect he had had. The girls watched him gradually disintegrate until he just gave up; gave up getting up in the morning, so he got the sack, and that gave him the excuse to lie in bed all day; gave up shaving and keeping himself clean; gave up finally struggling with his health and the disease in his lungs took over and they watched him being taken off to the clinic in Surrey Hills. They were not allowed to go up to his ward. They were children. Only BB, coming onto the scene again in a flush of compassion was allowed up to his room. She told them he wouldn't even look at her. And Josie knew the pain of her return hastened his end. BB pushed him out onto the balcony one last time in his wheelchair where he waved down to them feebly as they stood staring up from Crown Street. It didn't seem like him anymore thought Josie. More real than his death was the awful stench of the Toohey's brewery she remembered as they walked sadly down the hill to Central Station to catch the train to Circular Quay.

So BB came back, sans journalist for a while, and thought she could pick up from where she had left off, as though their life was a piece of knitting that she had discarded and she was now ready to ply the needles again.

Years and years ago, all ancient history now thought Josie. But it still hurt when she thought about it. And all the hurt – for what? When BB did abruptly turn around and marry the journalist, the second marriage failed much quicker than the first. And her third and last marriage was even more brief.

Josie had come to the last fence before the river when a slight movement caught by the corner of her eye made her start, and three small wallabies suddenly bounded out from a shrub just ahead. She watched them jumping swiftly and gracefully over the grass and fallen trees and then clear the fence between the paddock and the river in one elegant leap, moving as one, pivoting sharply and disappearing over the sandy bank. The sight released her from her memories and she swung out, taking in the golden light of the sun, blazing still as it went down, casting long shadows on the dry earth. A wheeling flock of cockatoos soared over her, screaming to each other from their sulphur crested heads. White and yellow, they rose in a cloud from one pale tree to another; and then a squabble broke out and a black and white magpie, shrieking as it darted across the intensely blue sky, was attacked by twenty, thirty, forty birds, swooping and soaring above her in a cacophony of sound.

Alex will love it here she thought as she climbed over the fence at the corner of the paddock, using the stretcher post to hoist herself over. Wisps of greasy sheep's wool were caught on the barbed wire. She felt them with her fingers. How soft and crinkly the wool was. Oh yes, he would love it here. Her city child who equated space with freedom, an idea Josie knew to be false.

The river was low and the banks where it receded, sandy. Josie kicked off her sandals and ran towards the water where the sand had turned to mud. It oozed warmly between her toes. She longed for a swim and decided to go in in her underwear. No one was about, so she pulled off her skirt and shirt and threw them behind her on the dry sand. She waded in until the cooler ribbons of water around her knees told her the river was deepening and she threw herself into it and let herself sink. She dived deeper as she reached the pool at the bend but the water was dark and murky at the bottom with submerged tree trunks which brushed against her legs, and the thought of some giant Murray Cod doing the same brought her swimming quickly back up to the surface.

Josie swam back to the bank, feeling the tug of the current against her stroke, but today it was hardly anything, so sluggishly was the river flowing. She waded ashore and spread out her skirt and threw herself down on it to dry in the sun. She lay on her stomach listening to the pounding of the blood in her veins, her heart pumping, feeling the heat from the ground beneath her, the sun above her, and watching the sun's rays fracture in the prism of a drop of water on her arm. She felt at one with the water and the sand and the sun, as though they had created her. She was made of the same elements as themselves. For the first time since she left New York and had said goodbye to Michael at the airport, Josie felt relaxed.

With her head on her arm, Josie examined the grains of sand on the hairs of her forearm and tilting her head a little she could see above the banks her sister's house, sitting majestically, brooding and grey, on its own knoll of green. How she had once wanted that house. The upper windows with their blinds drawn and their awnings lowered, gave the house a hooded look, like a falcon with its eyelids sewn shut that she had once seen in a book. The house had looked just the same the first time she had seen it, when she and Liz had been invited down from Sydney to stay for the Picnic Races.

She smiled at the memory. It was Harry's sister Julie who had asked them to join a house party. Julie had invited Michael too, the American student, because he was so 'exotic' she said. By that she meant, Josie realized later, he was Jewish. Josie and Julie were friends. They were both students at the Beryozka Ballet School. They used to meet Liz after classes (Liz coming from her art lessons), and the three of them would pool their money and go to a Repins Coffee Shop in Darlinghurst Road and share a plate of mushrooms on toast. They would giggle over the present and create fantastic futures for themselves, futures gloriously spread before them, blank sheets to be written on.

That year, when the Royal Easter Show was on, Harry had come to town. Liz and Josie hadn't met him before though Julie was always talking about this good-looking brother she had who seldom left the farm. Julie took Josie along to see the agricultural display and the sheep entered from Tiddalik — but they both knew she was really taking Josie to meet her brother.

And Julie hadn't exaggerated in her description of him. He was a strikingly handsome young man, his skin and hair so sun-burnished from years spent outdoors, that even his eyelashes, Josie remembered, had glinted gold. He had an easy smile which he used often and it had a devastating effect on all the girls he met.

Tiddalik had taken a third place ribbon for its wool, and to celebrate, Harry and his sister took some friends out to dinner. Michael was with them then, and Liz. They had all squeezed into a taxi and gone zooming up William Street to the Cross; the neon lights at the top seemed to be winking them on.

It was then and there, jostling against each other in the rattling taxi, like coloured pieces in a kaleidoscope, that Josie believed fate decided to play with their lives; hers and Harry's and Liz's.

In the city streets, Harry had seemed uneasy, crushing his soft, wide-brimmed country hat between his hands. But when they came down to Tiddalik for the Picnic Races in the local country town, with their best dresses packed carefully in their weekend portmanteaus, Harry had seemed to fit the landscape as a tree its bark. The awkwardness he had shown in Sydney, attractive as it was, was here replaced with a comfortable oneness with the land around him. He had an easy grace about him, a slow, sure way of moving that was surprising in a man so large. Whether with the animals, or saddling his horse, or laughing and telling yarns with his country friends, or showing them, new city folks, his prowess with a bull whip, Harry had a charm about him that both Josie and Liz had succumbed to. Even Michael had found Harry's friendship hard to resist. The year of the Picnic Races, Josie remembered, the cherry trees had been laden and Harry's mother had asked him to go out and scare the birds away.

43

He had uncurled the long stock whip and cracked it so easily and effortlessly, the cracks repeating like rifle shots around the valley that Josie, watching from an upper window had wondered how strong his arms would be. Old Mrs Barton had caught her looking out the window at her son and Josie had blushed and withdrawn her head.

It was that weekend thought Josie lying beside the river bank twelve years later, that the loose shapes of coloured glass imprisoned between the mirrors, like the sun in a drop of water on her arm, had shifted and settled, and Liz had confided in her that she had fallen in love with Harry. The memory made Josie shift uncomfortably and an ant crawled over her fingers and bit her. Josie spat on her finger and rubbed it with sand.

They had driven off to the races the next morning, leaving behind them the massive grey stone house, festooned with wisteria and ivy as though it mocked its own impressiveness. The hamper in the trunk of the car had been filled with picnic fare; homemade bread cut into thick rounds with slices of tender Tiddalik lamb; jars of pickled walnuts from the old trees in the orchard; bottles of mustard and relish, champagne and ginger beer. Crystal glasses were carefully wrapped in linen napkins and slabs of boiled fruit cake, moist and spicy with marzipan and royal icing, were packed beside a fragile, high, pale sponge cake filled with farm cream and mulberry preserves. In the lid of the hamper, plates, and knives and forks with ivory handles were stored. The sight of such abundance and rare and beautiful things impressed both Liz and Josie.

It had rained on and off that day and they had all had too much to drink. The champagne had become warm and sticky and their straw hats were soaked and they spent most of the day getting in and out of the car to repair the damage to their hair, or their muddy feet. By evening, the country roads were a quagmire. There was a great deal of pushing and jollity to get the big old Humber, which Harry called Bertha, out of the mud in the field where they were parked. And when they were on the road they had crept along within the cone of their headlights while the rain continued to fall. Julie, who insisted she was the most sober, was driving, with Michael and somebody else beside her, and Liz and Harry and Josie had squeezed into the back with a Pete or Peter, who was dead drunk, lying across their knees.

They were all singing snatches of songs and peering through the deluge, for the clouds had now really opened up and they were wishing the ride would never end, for the excitement and closeness of their young bodies made them dimly aware of the transcience of all things. The rich smell of wet grass on their shoes, the smell of damp starch running from the girls' limp dresses, the whiffs of champagne and tobacco, all mingled with the old leather scent of the seats. It was an elixir to their fuzzy minds as they passed another bottle of champagne from one to another. They swigged it straight down and it filled their mouths with foam.

'A toast! A toast!' shouted Harry.

Liz shrieked, her inhibitions loosened like the bubbles flowing down the neck of the bottle.

'To what Harry? To what?'

'To . . . to Fortuna!' he shouted, leaning over her and winding down the window, and then pulling off her hat as she shrieked again and flattened herself against the seat as the rain and wind spattered her. He held her hat out in the dark howling night like a cup held up to the gods.

'To Fortuna,' he shouted into the rain, 'That we may always recognize her when she rains down – and catch her when we do.'

He fell back laughing between them and dumped the wet hat on his head. He took a swig from the bottle and then his eye caught Josie's and they burst out laughing at how ludicrous he looked with her sister's hat on his head. And then suddenly in the midst of their laughter he kissed her firmly on the mouth and she was surprised how fresh he tasted. And over his shoulder she could see Liz fiercely winding up the window. It was as though a frame in a movie had been frozen in Josie's mind for she saw it often after that whenever she thought about Liz, long after she had married Michael and Liz had married Harry; a picture of her sister winding up the car window, closing in the sides of the car, as though through the window they could all be sucked out into some uncontrollable and unknowable void.

It had been the first lie, that little kiss.

Josie could see it now, looking back. Everything grew from that. How simply and innocently our mistakes are made, she thought as she stood up and brushed the sand from her legs and arms. She stepped into her crumpled skirt and buttoned on her shirt.

She wondered what Harry was like now? She had not seen him since the wedding – his wedding to Liz, when she, the younger sister was the bridesmaid. Josie had not been back to Australia since then. Six weeks after her sister's wedding in Australia, Josie had married Michael in New York. How different their weddings had been: Liz's here in the garden, with a marquee and flowers, and lots of Barton relations and friends, and even a photographer from the Australian *Women's Weekly* to record the social event: her own in the quiet, empty Brotherhood Synagogue in Greenwich Village.

Josie was nervous about seeing Harry again. She was unsure what her feelings about him were. It was the reason she had come back. The reason she kept quietly to herself. Michael suspected it. No, she was sure in fact that he knew. She could not hide it completely from him; her own dissatisfaction with their marriage, her own restlessness. She had to find out about herself. Once and for all she had decided to face up to the truth, about her true feelings for Harry. Was it a girlish infatuation which she should have forgotten long ago? Was it all over? Had it all been a lie? It seemed so silly to feel so strongly about an emotion twelve years old. But in her case it was the most real thing she knew.

Michael, who seldom shouted, had snapped at her once, 'You're no better than your mother.' And she had reacted as though she had been slapped; 'Don't say that to me!' The intensity of her reply had frightened her. She had brooded over it. If it were true. She had tried so hard to be better than BB; a better wife; a better mother. And increasingly as she watched Alex grow up and her own career promises fade, her life settling into a pattern not of her own choosing, she felt that she was living a lie. That it was threatening to choke her. And all the time she wondered if the reason was because she was like BB.

And there was the other problem.

Liz. Her feelings about Liz.

Here on Harry's land, on her sister's land, their land as far as the eye could see in all directions, Josie felt a fraud. A cheat. That was why she had felt so uncomfortable in BB's house; sitting there silently while BB worked out how to tell Liz of *her* latest deception. And all the time Josie had sat there, holding in her own secret, watching BB wrestle with hers. They had both sat there like – like frogs. It had to be true. In all the wrong things she was like her mother. Whom had she been kidding all these years? At times it was like having a ferret inside you tunnelling away at all the good.

Josie put on her sandals. Alex would be awake by now. She could no longer put off seeing Harry. Her stomach knotted. How she despised herself. When she looked up from buckling on her sandals, the world was just the same, still aloof, unconcerned. The sun was glinting in long low brush marks across the tops of the far hills, and the river and the immediate valley where she stood were in shade. The sky was

47

now a deep ink blue on the horizon, as though a storm were coming, but there was not a breath of wind.

Josie climbed up the bank heading for the front drive. She turned around for a moment and caught a last glimpse of her mother's house. She thought she could see the blue of her mother's dress in the garden against the gold hues of the dying sun. But she could not be sure and she set off for the front drive that lay like a pale arrow pointing the way to the people in the Big House.

· FOUR ·

After an early supper of mutton neck chops and peas, BB was sitting up in bed with a single forty watt bulb burning beside her attracting every gnat and flying insect within Tiddalik's boundaries. The windows were flung open to the night and despite the screens the tiniest mites got through and thickly congregated around the lamp, living, loving, and dying in the space of a few hours between the bulb and the shade.

On the bed with her, BB had one of her boxes, Eta Peanuts. 16 ozs. It was full of letters, and postcards and photographs. She was sucking on a quartered orange while she riffled through them. She had become sentimental as she grew older, and her memory, like the hills of Tiddalik, was fading at the edges. She held a letter up to the light, rubbed a juice stain with her finger.

1942.

Darling BB,

I think of you all the time. I cannot get you out of my head. What have you done to me? I wish I could tell you where I was – though I think you can guess. Even in the funk holes I think of you – your white legs – your urgency. Remember that night when we couldn't find a room and you didn't want to take me home? Ah BB you make the war seem unreal. But the Australian fighting man is something to be seen. Even if you *do* speak with a pommy accent, you're one of us now. If I were younger

I would throw away this typewriter and join them. Yesterday I saw a troop train pulled up, full of hundreds of men. The Malay kids were screaming at them, Hello Joe. Hello Joe. God, it made you proud just to . . .

Enough of that, thought BB, dropping the letter on the floor. You don't have to tell me the attraction of a uniform.

1950.

Dear Mum,

I'm so excited. We're having a baby! Michael thinks it's great – thank God. I don't know what I'd do if he didn't. He's so kind to me, really Mum. It makes up for his parents. I knew I was expecting even before the doctor told me. I've had this strange tingling in my breasts. Quite strong enough to be uncomfortable at times. It is like an effervescence. It made me think of Eno's Fruit Salts except it's under my skin. Did you have that feeling with me? You never talked about us as babies. We have one spare room we've used for storage that we will make into the nursery. It has a nice window overlooking the street. If I stick my head out I can just see the corner of Carl Schurz Park. I'll take the baby there for walks. Can you come and see us? Michael says . . .

Michael. I never did think much of him. No back to his head. Always worried me that – his head went straight down into his collar. Thick, I thought, though Liz says on the contrary he's very smart. Look at this wedding picture she sent me. What a pretty thing she was. Funny wedding though from what she told me. Stamping on a glass. Funny people.

1950.

Dear Josie,

Whenever I hear of domestic disasters in America, I imagine all sorts of things! Can you sleep at night? The whole world is in a proper mess. I wish we could give it up. We could join that American sect that refuses to accept the 20th century! All we would need is a bonnet and a cape, and a cuddy to stay in. And no husbands thank you! I don't know why I ever married this man. After this, no more romantic interludes – and I'll stay clear of LEOS. They are poison to me. Each man in my life to date was born in the first week of August! Boy! If ever I meet a wealthy Western District grazier I'll ask him his birthdate first. The news about the baby is wonderful. But I can't see myself as a grandmother. Perhaps that's all the use I'll be when I get rid of *him*. I've rented a flat, but the stairway is tortuous. I don't think my new 'fridge will get up there. He's not getting it, that's for sure. When I work it out, *then* I'll divorce him . . .

I wonder why I've still got this letter? The envelope's been to New York and back. RETURNED FOR INSUFFICIENT POSTAGE. BB sucked on her orange. What a waste of time writing that letter was. And this one? How did this get in my box?

Artificial insemination is an easy process in cattle, for the semen can be frozen in straws to be used months later if necessary. Sheep semen does not freeze as well and for this reason a live ram is used. After the ewe has been marked as being in season by a teaser ram . . .

BB turned the paper over. It was one of Harry's pamphlets. Everything seemed to end up in BB's boxes. BB put her hand up delicately under her chin and spat out an orange pip. A thud from above her ceiling told her the 'possums were back. BB put the pip on the night table where the tiny insects were so thick that she could draw a finger through them as though they were dust. When she went back to her riffling she came

to a sheet of lined school paper with large childish writing –
from Josie or from Liz?

Why did you go away? Pleese come back. We miss you.
Dad says you're never coming back. Is that true? I promis
we will be good. I am sorry I told lies and made you
unhappy. I reely didn't mean it Mum. Will you be home
for my birthday? I hate this place. If you don't come
home I'll hate you. I hate you. I hate you . . .

That was Liz.

1953.

Dear Mrs Beauchamp,

I have just read your ad in *The Times* and I believe you
and I may be first cousins. My Aunt Daphne had a baby
girl given up for adoption in 1911. Could that baby be
you? Could you telephone me? I will be in London to
see the Coronation next week. We could meet then . . .

——A yellow telegram.

1953.

MRS BETTY BEAUCHAMP URGENT YOU CALL OR WRITE
STOP JOSIE SERIOUSLY ILL NEW YORK HOSPITAL STOP
COME IF YOU CAN STOP MICHAEL ROSENBLOOM

And another.

1953.

PLEASE FORWARD TO MRS BETTY BEAUCHAMP URGENT
SHE CONTACT JOSIE NEW YORK HOSPITAL STOP SERI-
OUSLY HURT IN CAR ACCIDENT STOP APPRECIATE PROMPT
REPLY STOP MICHAEL ROSENBLOOM

What a busy year that was, going to London and meeting
my own mother. BB threw the telegrams up in the air and

watched them flutter onto the bed. I could only do it because of the divorce and being granted the house. Liz kept calling that husband an undertaker. It used to make him furious. He was president of the Australian Cremation Association. I only went into his office once, in Rowe Street, and there were all those boxes, like shoeboxes, except they contained ashes, stacked on the shelves. The tea lady brought us some tea and there was some plaster dust on the floor and she screamed and dropped the tray and ran out of the door. It did make me laugh. But he had no sense of humour. Not Mr Hoity-Toity. Just as well I always kept to my first married name. Betty Beauchamp would do me. Not Mrs Sin-jin. He always said it that way and it was just plain old Saint John. I sold that house at a very good profit, come to think of it. I went by ship. Oh I do love the sea. That's what I miss most about living here at Tiddalik. I wonder if Daphne would like to see the sea? All that lovely money. It wouldn't cost much, a few days in Sydney near Balmoral or Manly.

1962.

BB Dear,

The Lawn Bowling Association is having a dance on Thursday night. Will you come as my partner? There will be Highland Flings and Eightsome Reels and all those things that you enjoy and do so well. I never can remember all the steps or which way I am supposed to turn. You make me feel young again BB and if it were possible it would be a great honour and comfort to me if you would consider being my partner more permanently. Whatever your answer, and please think about this most seriously, I hope to see you on Thursday . . .

Poor Mr Doughty, always a gentleman, and always boring.

53

1944.

You are a bitch BB. Don't ever come near me and the girls. We are doing just fine – no thanks to you. When you're thrown out by lover boy don't come running back here. We don't need you . . .

Ah. Mr B. He always did have a way with words. BB crumpled up the letter and then smoothed it out again. It was getting late and tomorrow they were going to collect Daphne. She rummaged through the box but couldn't find a picture of Daphne, but there was an old one of herself taken during the war. She supposed that was when she looked her best. She peered at the picture, flipped over the back. 1942. She must have been thirty, thirty-one then. Not bad looking. She looked closely at the photograph, it could have been a stranger, the smooth high forehead, the big brown eyes in the long face. Liz had once likened it to a Vermeer portrait she had seen in her art book. BB had been offended. But, she thought now as she stroked her throat, running her hand down over the now bumpy chest bones, lifting her fingers as she reached her nipples – she *had* been good-looking and had at least passed that on to her daughters. She hoped they appreciated it.

BB switched off her light. The farm was never really quiet and the 'possums thumped above her head. 'Go away,' she said sleepily, but they were nocturnal friends. The noise did not really disturb her because she knew what it was. The only drawback was that they peed up there and the stains came through the ceiling. As for eating her geraniums . . . Liz would never hear anything against her cat.

BB thumped her pillow into shape, closed her eyes and fell asleep.

· FIVE ·

'Hello, Harry.'

Josie was coming down the stairs at the Big House and met Harry and Liz in the entrance hall. The three of them stood smiling at each other under the hard light of the wooden chandelier. Harry moved first.

'Josie! You haven't changed a bit!' He hugged his sister-in-law to him and then held her at arm's length. 'Not a bit, has she?'

'No, hardly at all,' said Liz regarding her sister under the light. Her eyelashes and nose caused deep shadows on her face. It made her nose seem longer than it was. Harry's arms dropped and Josie touched her sister's arm nervously in greeting. A narrow silver bracelet on her right wrist shimmered.

'Oh yes I have,' she said looking at Liz, and then at Harry with a laugh. She had showered and changed after her swim and was wearing a pair of beige slacks and a silk shirt which showed her throat. In the hollow of her throat there was a small mole which she touched self-consciously as she looked at Harry. She spoke to Liz.

'Alex is awake. He'll be down soon.'

'You look so cool,' said Liz running her hands down the sides of her skirt. 'I think I'll go up and change for dinner. Harry, why don't you have a drink on the verandah and fix one for me too? A brandy and dry,' she said over her shoulder as she went up the stairs.

'You look well too, Harry,' said Josie when they were sitting outside with their drinks in their hands, a drinks tray with ice and glasses on a table between them.

'Cheers,' he said lifting his Scotch and looking at her over the glass.

She lifted her glass and looked out over the darkening garden, through the thick boughs of the wisteria to the river and the hills. She was very conscious of him, sitting in an old chair, his favourite no doubt, and she thought it looked a bit like the hills around them, worn and bleached. She looked back at him while there was still enough light. His face with its angular planes was very much as she remembered it. There were the two vertical lines between his eyebrows, deepened: the line of the mouth, firmed: the colour of his eyes light brown as the liquid in his glass. There *was* something different though that Josie could not quite pinpoint. Perhaps it was just the thickening blue shadows of the evening that were playing tricks with the light. Or perhaps; just age. It had been a long time. He echoed her thoughts in words.

'It has been a long time, Josie. It is good to see you again.'

He smiled at her and she could see the grooves in his cheeks. He raised his glass to her again, steadying an ashtray on the arm of his chair with his other hand. Ruby came and plopped down beside him.

She sighed and gave in to the beauty and tranquillity of the summer evening, a letting go, which, if she had been able to see herself, was reflected in the softening curve of her arm, the slight dropping of her lower lip.

'I still can't quite believe I'm here. I just made up my mind to come and arranged the tickets and took Alex out of school early . . .'

'Michael couldn't come?'

'No,' she paused, dipping her filter tip cigarette into her glass of gin. 'No, he's too busy.' She put the damp cool filter on her lips and drew the smoke through it.

'I've forgotten what business Michael finally settled on.'

'Corporate law.' She blew out the smoke. 'Tax specialist.'

Harry looked out at his land.

'Bit different from sheep's arses.'

'Not much,' she said.

They both laughed, the tension between them easing. Josie sat more deeply into her chair, touched a heavy pendulous bloom of the late flowering wisteria. A small mauve flower broke from its stem and fell into her glass. She picked it out with one finger and said, looking at it closely as though the tiny petals would reveal something to her, 'You know, when we got married, I thought Michael was going into his father's business. Did you ever meet Michael's father? No. Well, he's a nice little man, much more approachable than the formidable Mrs Rosenbloom. He was an exporter. I imagined my life with Michael would be one of travelling to exotic ports and buying beautiful things. Michael spent about a year at it, and most of that time he was in the seedier parts of Manhattan, moving between his father's warehouse and the custom's offices. The trouble was, he wasn't very good at it. The last straw for the old man came when Michael imported thousands of yards of metallic material from India. First they had to fumigate the warehouse because of the bugs in it, and then the manufacturer of the car seats Michael thought was going to use all this stuff, discovered that the material acted as though it had teeth when anyone in a fur coat sat on it.' Josie giggled at the memory. 'Soon after that Michael went to law school. His father helped us and we just couldn't have made it without him. He didn't want me for a daughter to begin with. A *schiksa* for his only son.' She smiled ruefully. 'I was working too to make ends meet, and then I had the accident. My pelvis was crushed in the car accident so I couldn't dance any more.'

'Michael wrote to me at the time. He blamed himself for the accident.'

'It was no-one's fault. We were driving down the Taconic

Parkway. It was May and we had spent the weekend with friends in their country house in Dutchess Country. It was just getting dark, a Sunday night, and a deer came right across the road. We hit it and spun out of control. Thank God Alex was strapped in his safety seat in the back.'

They were silent. She thought about that endless spinning motion that night, the sickening crunch of metal and the weight on her, the soft pine needles under her hair on the side of the road, the deep green firs she had seen before she passed out. She looked at the pale barked gumtrees on the present horizon and blinked.

'Do you ever get the feeling that you are in a painting and the light's all wrong, as though it's coming from the wrong source?'

'That's the kind of thing Liz would say, and I can't say that I do.'

'Well, it's hard to explain,' she ran her hands up her arms. 'Sometimes I feel I'm on a different wavelength from everyone else.'

'Well, you do have BB for a mother.'

She didn't smile.

'Now, *that*'s the kind of thing Liz would say.' She stood up and leaned on the curved stone balustrade of the verandah looking out at the clear dark night.

'Mum's house up there. She's a funny old bird, isn't she? I mean she's not like anyone else's mother that I know. Sometimes I wonder if I am only what she made me. Nothing to do with myself.' She turned around and sat on the balustrade facing him. 'I'm sorry to get so intense. BB does this to me. I thought I was over it. Grown up. But perhaps we never do get away, and carry them on our backs forever. You didn't get so tangled up in your mother's life, did you?'

'Oh Josie, you really haven't changed at all have you? You're still questioning and not content with what you have.' He laughed.

The blood rushed to her face and she was glad of the darkness. The only light apart from the moon came from the sitting room window falling in a rectangle on the quarry tiled floor.

Josie lightened her voice, trying to be flippant. She tapped another cigarette out of her packet.

'Am I really so transparent?'

'I've hurt you,' he said. 'I'm sorry, I didn't mean to.'

'No. No, you haven't,' she lied. 'It's easy for you. Men are allowed to overcome their fathers. It's part of growing up.'

The screen door onto the verandah banged.

'Mom, are you out here?' Alex's voice came from the doorway. Josie got up and went to the corner of the verandah to meet him.

'Alex, come and meet your Uncle Harry.' She brought him to Harry, so proudly, she could not help it, and introduced them.

'Alexander Rosenbloom. Harold Barton.' They shook hands, the boy shuffling from one sneakered foot to the other. He was tall for his age and his brown hair, though short, fell across his forehead just the way Josie's did. He pushed it back with his hand.

'Why, you're almost a man,' said Harry straightening himself to his full height and looking the boy over.

'I'll be *barmitzvahed* next year,' said Alex, the little boy in him winning the battle over whether he should be friendly or cool.

'I'm just an old cocky-farmer,' said Harry sitting down again and motioning Alex to do the same, 'so you'll have to tell me what that means.'

'It means,' said Josie, crossing over to her son and handing him an orange drink, 'that he will have to practise his Hebrew more or he'll never be able to recite his *maftir* correctly on the day.' She ruffled his head affectionately and remembered, at the sight of his embarrassment, how much he hated her to do that now that he was nearly grown.

59

The screen door banged again. Liz came around the corner of the verandah looking much cooler and younger with her hair brushed loose and wearing a white caftan that billowed around her as she walked. She was carrying a plate of cheese cubes and smoked oysters on round biscuits.

'Are you feeling more awake now, Alex?' she asked, picking up her glass of brandy and dry ginger ale from the tray. She took a sip and then added more ice to it.

'Yes, thanks, Aunty Liz.'

She offered him the plate.

'Gosh, I'm starving, aren't you? Don't eat those grey things, no one under thirty likes them.'

Alex nibbled carefully at a cheese cube.

Liz sat down with a grateful sigh with her back against the wall of the house. There were times when the sisters looked alike, when Liz's face was more relaxed and the tension that sometimes showed around her eyes eased.

With Josie, the face was all curves, the high cheekbone, the round eye, the full soft lips, which, even when pressed together looked plump. In Liz, all these features were elongated. She bit into an oyster with her long white teeth.

'What have you been talking about?'

'We were talking about the role of women and the role of boys,' said Harry with a smile at Alex.

'What about the role of women?'

'Josie thinks men have it easier because we are able to kill off our fathers and women aren't able to kill off their mothers. Figuratively speaking that is of course. This has nothing to do with BB.' They all laughed and he stood up and poured another drink for himself and Josie.

Alex was looking bored. Harry noticed it and sitting down again leant forward on his knees and said to the boy: 'What I want to know Alex, is what a *maftir* is?'

Alex shot him a grateful look; at last there was something he could talk about.

'It's a reading from the Torah. Dad and I have been practising. I have to read it in the synagogue and all our friends come and afterwards there's a big party with presents and everything. Will you come? Can they come, Mom?'

'They might,' she smiled.

Josie was watching her son as he talked, his hands making the same gestures that she herself used. At times it seemed to her that she had conceived him on her own. He had none of his father's features. He was indeed nearly a man. She listened to them talking and she thought about it while the darkness of the Australian bush crept closer to the house. Alex as a man. His *barmitzvah* would show that; that in all ways he was ready to assume his future as an adult Jew. He hadn't fought going to Hebrew School after his usual classes ended and in fact seemed to enjoy struggling with the black squiggling letters that read from right to left. Liz had always enjoyed intellectual pursuits more than herself.

In their small apartment in Manhattan, Josie would hear Alex and Michael practising in another room, with the door shut, and she would pause and listen to the ancient sing-song of the voices, a murmuring humming she could not understand. There was Michael's deep voice and Alex's treble, hesitating, accompanying him. It made her feel an outsider, standing there at the painted door with the chrome handle with her dishcloth in her hand; both as a woman and a non-Jew.

While she was pregnant with Alex she had attended a *bris* in the apartment of one of Michael's friends. She had found the whole ceremony foreign and barbaric. Josie's father, who came from Britain, had not been circumcised; but many Australian men were. It was a matter of hygiene. Josie had felt this circumcision was barbaric only because it had been done there in the bedroom, on the bed where the young couple slept, with all their friends and relatives crowded into the tiny walls of the apartment. and when the *mohel*, the professional circumciser, had spread the baby flat like a chicken on a board, and the boy's grandfather had held the little legs, she had felt ill and held her own swollen belly softly in her hands. She had listened to the intonement: 'Blessed are you Lord our God, Master of the Universe, who have made us holy with your commands, and have commanded us to bring this boy into the covenant of Abraham our father'. Josie, who had been brought up firmly by the nuns to believe in the Trinity made a silent prayer to Jesus.

When Alex was born at Mt Sinai Hospital some weeks later, the *mohel* would not attend because Josie was not a Jew, and the circumcision had been performed by their own doctor. But the approaching *barmitzvah*, and Hebrew School, Josie thought, they were something else. Now that Alex was attending Hebrew School, Michael was putting pressure on her to convert. 'Listen,' he told her, 'the rabbi is very reluctant to perform the *barmitzvah* unless you do – you have to do it for Alex and me. I'm not going through the same milk-toast ceremony as I did for our wedding.' 'What was wrong with it?' 'A reform–rabbi makes me feel like a – a Protestant!' 'But why should I be converted? What difference does it make? I wasn't Jewish when Alex was born.' 'And the rabbi says he will overlook that if you convert when Alex is *barmitz-vahed*. It's a simple matter of some instruction.' A simple matter she thought now as she sipped her gin slowly and looked at her son as he talked with Harry.

They were talking about the farm and Harry was beginning to explain about his sheep and the breeding programme. In quite a scientific way, not talking down to the boy, he was explaining that by keeping one mob of a hundred as a control, and fitting the other mob of a hundred with hormonal devices he could judge more clearly the effects of the hormones on the sheep's fertility. A loud cowbell clanged metallically from the depths of the house and Liz jumped up and said, 'Thank God, saved by the bell.' And Harry sighed deeply and they all stood up.

Liz took the drinks tray and asked Alex to open the door for her. Josie and Harry stood for a moment putting out their cigarettes in the ashtray. Josie listened to the Australian countryside, the pained sounds of the bellowing cattle, sheep bleating, dogs barking, the incessant chatter of the cicadas in the great blackness. There was not a light to be seen in the whole darkness except from the window behind them and the large moon beyond the ghost gum on the lawn. It had been a very long day. It had begun for Josie and Alex in Hawaii, and Josie felt suddenly dizzy with fatigue, and disorientated, and very lonely. Suddenly very lonely. She was conscious of Harry's hand touching hers as they used the ashtray on the armchair. She could not be sure if his touch was accidental. She held her breath.

'Tired?' he asked.

'Yes.'

His hand came up and touched her face, and turned her chin towards him. She could only see his eyes very dimly in the darkness as he bent and kissed her gently on the mouth. It was as light as a finger brushing over her lips. He drew back and she looked at him and in the light from the window she recognized in his eyes what she had noticed and been unable to identify before. It was pity.

'We must go in,' he said.

'Yes.'

They crossed the rectangle of light and Ruby padded after them and they rounded the corner of the verandah and went inside.

No sooner had the flydoor banged shut than from the clump of rhododendron bushes beside the verandah, Jim stepped forward. He had woken from his drunken sleep with a very full bladder and had staggered out into the garden to relieve himself. He buttoned himself up slowly and stared at the lighted doorway for a few minutes, then he turned, scratching the back of his neck, and went towards the back of the house to wait for Cynthia to finish and take her home.

63

· SIX ·

The following morning, as was his habit, Harry got up at six o'clock, went down and opened the back door to let Ruby out, urinated on the lemon tree and splashed his face and hands with water from the garden tap. He went into the kitchen and lifted the chrome lid on the hotplate of the Aga and put a kettle on to boil. Then he went upstairs to shave, shower and change and was back in the kitchen in ten minutes to make his usual breakfast; grapefruit, Weetabix, strong tea and raisin toast.

Alex came in fully dressed, as he was sitting down to the table.

'Hello, old man. You're up early. Want some breakfast?'

'I couldn't sleep,' said Alex who was still on New York time.

'Want to come with me when we've eaten?' asked Harry putting three spoons of sugar into his tea.

Alex's eyes lit up.

'Sure. I'd love to.'

The boy tucked into a plate of Weetabix. Harry put some extra bread into the toaster.

'Got to keep your strength up then,' he said through a mouthful. 'Can you ride?'

'A little.' Alex bit his lip at this sign of his own timidity.

Harry smiled and seemed not to notice. They finished their breakfast in companionable silence and after Alex had left a note for his mother telling her where he had gone, they picked up some sandwiches from the refrigerator, 'plenty here for two of us', and they went out. On the verandah they paused while Harry found a felt hat to fit Alex.

'It's a bit ramshackle but it will keep the sun off.'

They crossed the back lawn passing under the giant gums and their cascade of wisteria and wild roses and Ruby followed behind them. They came to a small garden wall with two steps and Harry checked the rain gauge, though he knew, he said to Alex, it would show nothing. It did. He dropped the white tin contraption back on the stone wall.

'I'm always an optimist,' said Harry, 'but my God this has been a dry summer.'

'Isn't there any rain coming?' asked Alex quickening his step to keep up with his uncle's stride.

'Nope, and even if it did, the ground's so dry now, it would probably wash away the little bit of picking that is left.' Harry squared his hat on his head as though he were going into battle.

In the dusty circle in front of the stable block, Jim, his eyes bleary but otherwise recovered from his drinking bout, and Reilley, the only other man on the place, were hooking up a trailer to the back of the tractor. In the trailer were two large black oil drums. Jim touched his hat to Harry, as did Reilley. It was a gesture that was polite without being servile. They both nodded at Alex.

'Where are you off to?'

Harry stood with his hand on his hips. He was as rail thin as either man but a good head taller. Alex tried to imitate his stance.

Jim pushed his hat further back on his head so that his forehead showed a pale strip of skin above his sunburnt face. His face was as lined and grooved as his old leather R. M. Williams boots.

65

'Me cobber's going down the river, Boss, to Squatter's with some poison.'

Harry lifted the lid off one of the drums and Alex looked inside. It was full of carrots.

'How much did you use?'

'About a pint to every ninety pounds,' Jim said.

'Well, that ought to bloody do it! Reilley, watch you don't miss any openings now. I saw seven active warrens in Squatter's last week. There must be hundreds of bloody rabbits and their kittens down there. Eating their heads off they are.'

'Right, Boss.' Reilley hopped on the tractor and whistled his dogs to follow. He tossed his head at Alex. 'Nipper want to come?'

'No thanks, Reilley. He's coming riding with me.'

Reilley waved his hand and started the tractor. Harry shouted after him: 'And keep the dogs away from any carcasses.' He turned to Alex, 'That 1080 poison gets them every time.'

'It's dangerous, isn't it?'

'Not if we're careful.'

Alex gave Ruby's head a rub. The dog slavered over his hand.

Harry spoke to Jim about the day's plans.

'You'll get the killing done today, right?'

'I reckon.'

'And tomorrow we'll round up the wethers, right?'

'Reckon.'

'And Friday's the sale?'

'Hmmmm.'

'And Jim – lay off the booze, OK?'

Jim's mouth closed altogether. He scratched his head under his brim with one finger.

Harry waited.

'Jim?'

'Whatever you say, Boss.'

Harry made a snorting noise which was halfway between forgiveness and disbelief.

'OK then, Alex and me, we're going to check the pump up at Kurrajong. That dam's bloody low up there. I might have to move the breeding ewes if the water in the troughs is too low.' He said to Alex: 'Come on. You can ride my old horse, Trumps. He's good and steady and won't give you any trouble. He needs a bit of exercise.'

Harry then turned to his dog.

'No Ruby, you can't come today. We're going too far. Go home.'

Ruby slunk across the dusty circle and dropped mournfully and obediently under the gums, her eyes accusing her master of gross neglect.

Harry and Alex walked into the stable where the smells of horse, and manure, and hay and old sweat, assailed their nostrils. They went through the stable into the tack room where the saddles and bridles hung neatly on wooden frames nailed to the stone walls. Harry gave Alex a saddle cloth and told him which saddle and bridle to take. He picked up his own as if it had no weight at all and Alex staggered behind him to the yards at the back. In a small holding pen three sheep bleated feebly.

'Why are they in here on their own, Uncle Harry?'

'They're killers,' said Harry, 'part of the flock we keep for killing for meat on the farm. Each family gets half a sheep a week. Jim will kill them this morning.'

Harry threw his saddle across the top rail of the fence and Alex followed suit. Harry walked up to his horse, standing in the yard, and put on the bridle in one easy motion. The black velvet nose nuzzled his shoulder.

'This is Polo,' he said, patting the horse. 'Come and hold him for me while I put on the saddle.'

Alex did as he was told, standing a little back as his uncle threw the saddle cloth and the saddle onto the horse's back and tightened the girth strap with his knee in the horse's belly.

'Alex, I want you to wait here while I go and get Trumps. He's just in the next paddock.'

He took the spare bridle and swung into the saddle. Alex wished he could mount a horse like that. He opened the creaking gate of the stockyards and let his uncle through.

'Won't be a minute,' shouted Harry as he kicked Polo into a gallop and pounded over the paddock in a small cloud of dust.

Alex climbed onto the top rail to watch. He could see his uncle racing towards a group of three or four horses grazing in the far corner of the paddock. I like it here, I like the openness of the blue sky and the early morning air and the sound of the sheep and the birds. He thought sadly for a fleeting minute about his father getting up in the dark morning of a New York winter and leaving the apartment to catch the subway to Wall Street. This was better. He picked up a stone and idly chucked it into the pen where the three sheep huddled. They bleated and ran blindly into each other in panic.

'Hey, don't excite them.' Jim's voice, right at his ear, made Alex jump. Jim's hand rested on the wooden rail beside Alex's leg. Alex looked into the watery eyes. He was not sure if he liked Jim or not. He felt he was capable of things he wouldn't like to know about.

'Sorry,' he said.

'OK,' said Jim brusquely, letting himself into the pen and closing the gate behind him. 'If you excite them, see, it makes the meat tough. You want them calm, real calm.'

It was the most words Alex had heard Jim speak and his voice was a slow drawl. Alex was still listening to the words and the unfamiliar rhythm of Jim's speech when Jim quickly caught the sheep nearest him as it went past. He turned it over in the same movement and held it firmly between his knees. The sheep quivered with fear, the four legs trembling in the air and it bleated louder than ever. Jim squeezed it tighter with his legs, cursing under his breath, and holding its head back with one hand so that the throat was exposed, took with his other hand a sharp, long knife from a leather sheath at his belt. With one clean plunge into the neck he found the carotid arteries. It was all so quick that Alex almost missed the movement of his hand. A fountain of blood gushed out and the animal jerked and quivered as its muscles went into a spasm. Jim grasped the sheep's nose with his left hand and grabbed the wool above its eyes with his right; a quick pull up with his left hand and a thrust with the heel of his right, and there was a distinct crack as the atlas joint at the base of the neck broke.

Alex watched in fascinated horror as the blood was absorbed into the dusty earth, so dry and thirsty that the blood did not pool. Some green stuff began to come out of the throat. Alex couldn't look any more and turned his head away. He heard the sound of hooves and saw his uncle heading back across the paddock leading a fat grey horse at a steady trot. He opened the gate for his uncle, keeping his eyes away from Jim and what he was doing to the sheep and trying to keep his tumbling thoughts away from his queasy stomach.

When Trumps was saddled and Harry had helped Alex on and adjusted the stirrups till they were a comfortable length, Alex allowed himself one last sideways look at the killing yard. The three sheep now hung upside down, 'S'-shaped stainless steel hooks pushed through their hind legs above their hooves. They swung like pendulums and the soft sound of blood dripping into the dry earth was quite clear. Alex's gorge began to rise again but Harry said to him firmly: 'Now young Alex, keep your wits about you,' and showed him how to hold the reins and got him out of the yards and down the drive before he could vomit and make a fool of himself.

It was a beautiful day. The sky was the clearest blue and the air, not yet burnt by the sun, was fresh and thin. Alex soon relaxed; his hands grew less tense on the reins and his uncle's words of advice helped him loosen his back and settle into the easy rolling gait of Trumps's stride.

'Would you like to hear about my Dad?' said Harry in a conversational tone that made Alex realize he was about to hear a story.

'My Dad. I was scared to death of him.'

'You? Scared?'

'Yep. My brother Billy wasn't scared of him. But I was.'

'I didn't know you had a brother.'

'Billy died in the war. He was two years older than me. And my Dad loved him.' He paused and then was so silent that Alex turned around to look at him, but he was only staring ahead as they rode, his body relaxed, both reins in one hand, the free hand resting lightly on his thigh.

Alex kept quiet and Harry went on.

'It was Billy who taught me to ride. See the mailbox, way over there? At the front gate?' He pointed in the distance to a large green painted oil drum resting on its side on a cement block beside the main gates of Tiddalik. 'Billy used to race me there. He was fearless. He had a black pony called Midnight and it moved like the wind. That pony flew over the paddocks, and there wasn't a fence it wouldn't jump. Billy would shout, "Race you to the mailbox and back!" I can still see him shouting and laughing and racing that black pony, his hat flapping on his back and his arms and legs going like pistons. I used to trot more carefully behind him on my Shetland. One day up at Gully Paddock, our Dad had dug out a new dam up there, we were fishing for yabbies with chunks of rotten meat on strings.'

'What are yabbies?'

'Crayfish. Well, we weren't having much luck and Billy got tired of that, so he devised a game with a rope. We looped a rope over an overhanging tree and he would hang on it and I had to push him further and further out over the water until with a whoop Billy let go and fell in. Sometimes he made it, sometimes he didn't. He was covered in bruises always. He wanted me to do it, but I didn't dare.'

'What other games did you play?'

'Well, once we found an old abandoned water tank. It had been dumped in the gully when the new dam was finished. It was just a big corrugated drum like the ones back at the stables, except this one was rusted and corroded and the top and bottom were long gone. By standing inside and bracing ourselves we could rock the drum back and forth. It was great fun. And Billy decided we should take it higher up and we pushed it up the rise and took turns getting inside and pushing each other down the slope. But Billy was a daredevil. This was too tame and he wanted to try it from the top of the hill. So we tied the drum to our ponies' saddles and made them pull it up. They were skittering and frightened and jumping all over the place. At the top of the hill we untied the knots and rolled the tank into position and Billy straddled himself inside and braced his arms and legs against the walls.

'"Now when I say Go," he said to me, "you push." And then he shouted "GO" at the top of his lungs and I gave the tank an almighty heave and it began to tumble down the hill. At first it tumbled slowly and haltingly but then it gathered speed and rolled faster and faster until I realized it was going too fast and I had to stop it. I ran for my pony and jumped on not even stopping to put my feet in the stirrups. I saw the drum bouncing off the trees at the bottom of the hill and I saw Billy fly out like a rag doll of my sister's and lie absolutely still where he was thrown on the ground. The drum went careening on wildly and just – just crumpled when it hit a red gumtree that finally stopped it.'

71

'What happened?'

Harry eased himself in the saddle.

'I thought Billy was dead. His head was covered in blood and his eyes were closed. Billy. I kept shouting his name. He didn't answer. I got back on my pony and tore to the yards. It was so hot. I remember I couldn't see the rocks and trees for my tears and the sweat. I had never ridden so fast in my life. I ran to my father in the yards shouting and crying. My father was bending over the hoof of a horse with Jim. Jim was a bit younger then but not much different. They looked up and saw me and I saw my father look back at the horizon and then at me. I blurted out what had happened, that I had pushed Billy down the hill and that I thought he was dead. "Billy, I think I killed him," I said, "he's all bloodied and broken."'

As Harry spoke, Alex could imagine him as a child, could imagine himself standing in the dusty yards with the tears and the sweat running down his face.

'What did your Dad say?'

'He never said a word. His face turned white and I couldn't work out what was going on in his head. And then he raised his arm and I thought he was going to embrace me. But instead he swung back his arm and he struck me – a hard blow right across my face.' Harry put his hand up to his chin as though he could still feel the sting.

'But why?' asked Alex as they came to a gate and Harry pressed Polo's chest up close to it and bent to open it.

'Because he loved my brother more than me.'

'My Dad's never hit me,' said Alex clicking with his tongue to get Trumps to move through the gate.

Harry swung his horse around and closed the gate behind them.

'Nor should he. If I had a son I wouldn't hit him either.'

'He wasn't dead though, was he?'

'No, no. He had concussion and stitches in his head. He

thought it was a great lark. When he went off to the war, you could still see the scar. His hair never grew back along it.'

They rode in silence for a bit, each busy with their own thoughts, the sun rising higher in the sky absorbing even the sparse shadows thrown by the odd eucalyptus tree.

'It was Jim that comforted me,' said Harry into the silence.

They had been climbing steadily and loosed the horses' reins to enable them to have their heads more easily up the slope. They soon came to a wonderful high plain strewn with large and weird shaped rocks as though the earth at one time had convulsed and pushed up layers of its interior in vertical slabs. Ring-barked ghost gums stood in mute reminder of their long naked dying. Harry drew his attention to a mob of kangaroos that at first Alex couldn't see because their colouring blended in so well with the stones and shrubs. But then they moved and he watched with delight as they sprung away. Harry pointed towards a tree on the horizon and they headed that way, the horses picking their way carefully through the crumbling stones and low ridges of limestone that clicked and chipped against their hooves.

The tree they came to was an enormous Kurrajong that grew out of a great pile of thrust up stone and rock, its roots searching deep in the crevices for soil and nutrients to grow on.

'This is one of my favourite places on Tiddalik,' said Harry as he dismounted. They tied their horses to some bushes and Harry took out a canteen of water from his saddle bag. A few sheep picking through the rocks scurried away with a patter of hooves and a rattle of pea-like excrement. The cloud of flies which had lain on the horses all the way from the yards rose in confusion and then settled on the two humans. Harry ignored them. They climbed up the rock and stood under the spreading branches of the giant Kurrajong where they could see for miles in all directions.

'Is all this land yours?' asked Alex as Harry took out his

packet of cigarettes and sat down. Harry lit his cigarette, carefully extinguishing the match between his fingers and putting it back in his pocket. 'In case of bushfire,' he said, and then pulled on his cigarette and looked at the view, his elbows on his knees, the blue smoke curling lazily above him.

'Yes, it's all Tiddalik as far as the horizon. When my father was alive we had ten men full time on this place. Now we have two. It is beautiful, isn't it? I love this spot. It's a good place to come and think. See that shimmering over there? No. There? That's the house. Doesn't it all look small and insignificant from up here?'

'And there's the river,' said Alex as he caught the sun glistening on the narrow thread of water in the series of brown hills. He sipped some water from the canteen. It was warm but welcome.

'Is it ever green?' he asked, wiping his mouth with the back of his hand and passing the canteen back to his uncle.

'Only in the winter when we get the rain. *If* we get the rain.'

'There's not much for the sheep and cattle to eat is there?' said Alex looking at the sparseness of brown grass spread for miles around him.

'No. Not in a drought. Sometimes, when we're really desperate we can feed them these.' He pulled at an overhanging branch of the Kurrajong tree, showed Alex the leaves. 'They quite like it. But they don't get fat on it. This land could be so rich, so rich if we only had water. But you can't live on dreams. Better to use more wisely what we have.' He pulled at his cigarette, glanced at Alex who was sitting like him, with his knees up, hugging his legs and enjoying the space.

'Do you know anything about science?'

'We have it at school. We are doing biology this year.'

'That's one of the answers; biology. See those sheep over there? That small flock? We've kept them separate now from the rams for two months. We find now we can control their ovulation. Do you know what that is?'

Alex nodded as though he did and decided to ask his mother later.

'There's a bloke up in Sydney doing tremendous research into sheep fertility. He's a scientist at the University. He's got the right idea.' Harry put out his cigarette, rubbing it carefully against the rock, squeezing the butt and shredding it between his fingers. He put the fragments in his pocket.

'If this chap's right, and the experiments seem to show that, we can have all the lambs born in the season when we have most food and water. It gives them a better chance to survive, see? And what's better for the sheep is better for the farmer.'

Somehow this made Alex think of a line from a psalm he had read and he blurted it out without realizing he was speaking aloud: 'The earth is the Lord's and its fullness.'

Harry laughed and stood up and offered the boy a hand to pull him up beside him.

'You are a funny cove. Did your mother teach you that?'

'No. My Dad did.'

They climbed down to the tethered horses, Alex's legs feeling wobbly and stiff at the same time.

Harry helped him onto the horse and Alex winced when he felt the saddle underneath. His uncle roared with laughter, putting his head back and making the horses' ears prick up.

'We'll make a cowboy of you yet, Alex,' he said cheerfully. 'Let's go and see my ewes and then we'll check the pump and before you know it it'll be lunch time.'

· SEVEN ·

Liz was driving Josie and BB into Canberra to collect Daphne from the airport and do some last minute Christmas shopping. Liz had taken the white Holden station wagon, a car she never liked for she did not trust it. If it was not the carburettor, it was the spark plugs, if it was not the crankshaft, it was the brake. The car, Liz swore, had a mind of its own, but today she needed it because she wanted to pick up a Christmas tree, as well as the ham and the turkey and she expected that Daphne, coming to stay permanently, would also have a fair amount of luggage.

The car radio was on, one of the few things that did work, and they were listening to *Adeste Fideles* and *Jingle Bells* and Bing Crosby dreaming of a white Christmas, and it was ninety-three degrees in the shade. The vinyl covers of the seats stuck to their legs.

Liz had decided to take the back road to Canberra. This was little more than a dirt track running through neighbouring properties with five gates to be opened and shut and double that number of bone-rattling cattle-grids to be crossed. But it was still infinitely shorter to drive this way than the long way around on the bitumen road. It was also a more direct route to the north side of the city where her first stop would be at the butcher. Cynthia had also given her a long list of things she needed for the house; Josie wanted to visit a department store for some presents and wrapping paper;

and BB wanted to buy a block of Parmesan cheese and some semolina.

Liz knew she should not have asked, but she had asked 'Why?' before she could stop herself.

'For my gnocchi, of course,' BB had said on the phone that morning. Liz and Josie were eating breakfast at the table in the kitchen when the phone had rung.

'Well, thank goodness you've answered the phone at last,' BB had said petulantly.

'It's the first time it's rung, Mum.'

'Well, the cows must be leaning on the wires again, because I've been trying to get through for half an hour. Do you have any semolina, Liz? Hello?'

Liz held the phone out from her ear so Josie could hear the sound of their mother's voice tinnily coming through.

'I'm here. Don't shout. We don't have any but we can buy some. I'll add it to the list. I'll pick you up at ten.'

Liz put down the phone with a bang. 'I hope Daphne likes Italian cooking.'

Liz was feeling very snappish this morning. She had woken with a dull headache and it was still throbbing away behind her temples. She had not slept well and had woken from a dream, a dream she had not had for a long time. As a child she had believed that the night was a dark tunnel, a telescope, and that the moon was the daylight at the end. When she was small, she could fit into the telescope comfortably curled up, but as an adult the dream woke her in panic; she could not get out of the narrowing confinement; she was suffocating. Last night she had thrashed about with her arms and legs and Harry complained that she had woken him up. 'Sorry,' she'd whispered and lain awake till morning, feeling the sweat dry on her body and watching the dawn gradually open like the widening of some great lens.

The boiled eggs were ready and Liz brought them to the table, each one in individual crocheted caps. Josie raised her eyes at them and Liz groaned, 'I know they're awful but Mum made them and if I don't use them she'll notice.'

'In case you hurt her feelings?'

'No way. If I don't use them she'll probably make a whole lot more – and they may be even worse.'

Josie sliced the top off her boiled egg. 'Funny that she never taught us how to cook. She was always so good at it. I always associate her with food, somehow. Giblet gravy to meringues – she could do it all. Alex and Michael are lucky if I can open a packet of Twinkies for dessert.'

'She never taught us anything!' Liz said munching down two aspirins with a slice of toast and Vegemite. 'I take that back. The one thing she did teach me was how to sew press stud keepers into the shoulders of my dresses. So my bra straps wouldn't show. BB thinks sensuality was created only for her own indulgence; in her daughters, it was something to be denied.' She rolled her eyes and took a great bite out of her toast.

'Oh Liz, you're being a bit harsh.'

Liz uncovered her own egg from its little cosy, and her voice became serious as she tapped it with her spoon.

'You think so? Well tell me what she *has* taught us? By her example? No Josie, I'm not harsh. She never taught us a damn thing worth knowing. We brought ourselves up, you and me.' She stopped with her spoon in the air and said as though she hadn't thought about it before: 'You know something? I can't remember once, not once, being taken by her to something pleasurable, a cinema, an art gallery, a circus. Can you? Or a gift. Can you remember ever being given something special? Something you really wanted, that she'd thought about? What I would have given to have someone to share a book with. But never, never. What a waste my childhood was. Wasted by BB. I can't ever get that back. All I ever got were – egg cosies for God's sake. It was like being brought up by someone wearing rubber gloves with sandpaper on the fingertips so that everything that was done made one's nerve ends scream. She always gave me the feeling we were in the way, we were stopping her from doing what *she* wanted to do. Her career. A saxophone playing barmaid, the best in the world, she could have been if we hadn't been there. But she had to be there, some of the time, and she made me feel responsible. Can you imagine? She made me feel responsible for *her* difficulties when I was a baby myself.'

Josie spooned up her egg, the yolk dribbled down the side and she caught it with her finger and licked it. 'We haven't come out so badly though, have we?' She wished her sister wouldn't go on like this. It made her uncomfortable to be reminded of her debt to Liz. 'She must have taught us something worthwhile,' she said lamely.

'Whatever it was she probably didn't mean to. It would be something that just happened, a spin-off from something else. Accidental, like us.'

'But she was never physically cruel, Liz.'

'Of course not, she was much too apathetic for that. That would have meant she had to get involved with us. She had absolutely no mothering instinct.'

'I remember her sitting on the bed making us say our prayers at night.'

'Only when she remembered and was feeling guilty.'

'And we never missed Mass on Sundays.'

'*You* didn't. She did. Those mornings we used to walk to Mass when we missed the bus and we were terrified of burning up in hell. It was so vivid! So cruel to do that to children. I vowed I would never do that to my own. But then I never had to test it.'

Josie wiped her mouth with her napkin. 'What she used to drum into us though, was that sin would be punished.'

'Ha!' said Liz getting up from the table, 'I haven't noticed that in her case.' She walked to the sink with her dishes and saw through the window Cynthia walking slowly towards the house. There was something so dejected about Cynthia's walk that made Liz say: 'Oh, dear. Cynthia doesn't look too well today. I hope she makes it to the wedding.'

'When is it?' asked Josie who was still catching up with the farm's gossip.

'January sometime. She's bought the dress and everything. I was so cross with Jim when he did this to her.' She snatched a tea towel from the rack with an angry flick of her wrist. 'I could have cut off his balls.'

'I've a soft spot for that girl,' she said watching her and wiping her plate vigorously. 'She's just a big soft cow who could be used by anyone. She's got nobody. The nuns brought her up. Her father's a full blood, wherever he is, and country people can be such bitches to Abos. They won't even let her swim in the town pool.'

Cynthia came slowly into the kitchen through the verandah. She looked terribly tired. The heat and the baby were sapping her of energy.

'I feel real crook, Mrs Barton,' she said. 'I tried to call but the phone's out again.'

Liz put her hand on Cynthia's shoulder. For the first time that morning her voice softened. 'Cynthia, don't worry. If you'd just clear the kitchen for me now, we'll be fine by ourselves tonight. Go on. There's no one here today so it's a good time for you to rest up.'

The girl nodded miserably. Liz and Josie went to pick up what they needed for the day and Liz tried to put Cynthia out of her mind. The girl was like a great big purple plum with no skin and she needed a skin, one like Liz had developed, and it had to be tough. As prickly and hard as a lychee, so the sweet meat would be protected.

When Liz and Josie were dressed for town they went to the garage in the back garden. It was an ugly, utilitarian grey-painted tin shed trying to hide behind a fringe of honeysuckle. Inside, besides the station wagon, it contained an aluminium rowing boat on a trailer, and several tarpaulin covered objects like chairs and tables for the garden, screens and doors, and a lawnmower. Liz hooked back the swing doors while Josie looked around.

'What are these?' she asked, touching one of the packages wrapped in tarpaulin and tied with baling string leaning against the wall.

'Those? Oh, nothing. Just some old oils of mine. Not very good I'm afraid. Here, hop in.' She leaned over and opened the door for Josie.

'Don't you paint any more?' asked Josie getting in beside her, settling her floral skirt.

'No. Given all that nonsense up.' Liz slammed her own door and put the key in the ignition.

'You used to be quite good.'

'Quite good isn't enough.'

The car wouldn't start. Liz took the key out and inserted it again right side up. The engine coughed reluctantly and died. The car filled with petrol fumes. It seemed to Josie that her own thoughts were circulating with them. 'Flooded,' she said. They sat in the hot car for a minute, and in the forced intimacy Josie's voice blurted out, 'Liz, I must talk to you.'

'What about?' asked her sister, as if she didn't know.

'You. Me. Us.'

'Harry?'

'Yes. And Harry.'

'There's nothing to talk about,' said Liz turning the key viciously and being rewarded with a roar.

Oh dear, thought Josie, watching Liz pump the pedal, she doesn't want to hear. It was just the same when we were children sharing a double bed and we could tell what each other was thinking, and even then Liz would put up the barricades if I came too close. I could feel her stiffen in bed beside me, her cold toes withdrawing from me, the bones of her spine like a row of teeth saying get away, get away. So I was afraid to touch her. Just as I am now at the sight of her knuckles grasping the wheel, rows of white ridges I can never cross.

And her sister's bones talked to her and said, You are damn right I am not going to listen to you. Because what would I do if I did? Why should I let you put me in that position. To ease your guilt? To punish you? Don't put that burden on me Josie. You are grown up now, a woman too. Decide your own fate.

The child in Josie cried out, I don't want to hurt you, I don't. I love you.

And Liz's bones said to her, What a funny way you have of showing it.

Liz had caught her heel under the accelerator and she bent down to wrench it free and when she came up again she looked at her sister and said;

'There is nothing to discuss any more,' and, her eyes went on, it's time you accepted that; that you and Harry are old history. Like my paintings. Whatever there was between you before we were married is over. It was over a long time ago. He's mine now. You are no threat to me or him.

'Oh I wish life was more simple.' Josie wasn't sure if she were speaking aloud or not. I wish love was more simple. She fumbled with her bag looking for her sunglasses.

Liz had the car idling, nursing the juice with her pedal.

'It is simple if you want it to be. Don't get like BB.'

'This has nothing to do with BB.'

'Everything has to do with BB.' She put the car into reverse and twisted in her seat to back out. 'And in this case she's not going to win.'

Josie put on her sunglasses and retreated behind them.

As she drove, Liz wrestled with her thoughts. Her headache had come back. She had been trying to kid herself for weeks, ever since that phone call from Josie, that this was just a normal family visit – one nice sister visiting another. She had been weak to say yes. Weak. She hit the palm of her hand against the steering wheel as she thought about it. But she had buried her head, gone along with this subterfuge and ignored what was so obvious. Josie still loved Harry. But the trouble was, Liz did too.

She did not want Josie at Tiddalik. Liz was not as sure in her heart as she would have liked to be. Josie *was* a threat, a threat to all of them. Twin cords of jealousy and fear tightened in her stomach as she drove up to BB's house with the river on her left, she could just make it out behind her sister's profile. Her life, it seemed to her, was like this river. On the surface, the Murrumbidgee flowed smoothly, at times the water moving so imperceptibly westward, that you would swear it had stopped. Yet underneath, the currents picked up and tumbled, stones, trees and roots. Some mornings, looking out the front windows of the Big House, you could see great chunks of land torn away from the river bank, and only the branch of a stringy-bark or a red gum thrusting out of the water, would mark another victory of water against stone, patience against power.

Their marriage was like that too she thought, patience against power, rippling surface covering whirlpools. In a marriage of any length, Liz believed, love and hate were reconcilable. She could switch from one to the other with equal honesty in the space of days, even hours. It had taken her years to come to this maturity about love. There were times when Harry had hurt her. He had been unfaithful to her, twice that she knew of and probably more. And there had been times when she wondered why they were still together. But there was never enough hate to warrant getting out. She had seen BB make such a mess of her life, had suffered herself because of it, that Liz's one ambition in life was to keep her marriage together – at all costs. She did not feel compromised by this and she was not always unhappy

83

for she genuinely loved Harry. But she realized that part of that love was her commitment to it.

They had come to Top House in complete silence and BB got into the back seat of the car carrying a jam jar full of roses from her garden, 'to give to Daphne', she said, and wearing a cotton dress she had made herself with youthful puff sleeves.

'Aren't these blackboys beautiful,' she said as the heavy scent of the roses filled the car. She placed the jar carefully between her feet. 'Oh, I am so excited about today. Do you remember when I went over to England for the Coronation and found her?'

'You used your alimony money.'

'I know you never approved, Liz, but it was worth it. You can't always be sensible. When I finally met her, I wept into her coat. It was a red coat and it smelt of cat urine. She loves cats – you have that in common, Liz. We spent the whole day in my hotel room sucking ginger snap biscuits we'd dipped into our tea.

'There were so many things we found we had in common that made up for all those years when I felt so odd, so different from my parents. They were Italian. They got excited. I did not. How they made me suffer. They did like me, I think, until their own son came along. Marco. My baby brother. Everything changed when he came. You would think no-one had ever had a baby before. I had to be so good when they had guests. They all came to peer into the bassinet making goo-goo noises at this little dark baby. He had a lot of hair. My mother had decorated the nursery for him. It was all fresh and new. How I hated that wallpaper with its little flowers and cherubs sitting on swings. One day I stood up against the wall and when the guests came in and all their attention was on the baby, I peed against the wallpaper, all over my white socks and black shoes. It left a mark on the wall. My mother would point it out to people for months after that, until it was done over, the stain on the wall where I had disgraced myself over Marco.'

They had turned out of the main drive of Tiddalik and were driving now through a heavily wooded culvert, where, after heavy rain, a swift stream could close the road. Under the gums and river-oaks, between the splashy patches of the tree trunks, birds were swooping. The few remaining pockets of water kept their presence in this area. Small, vivid parrots and lorikeets dived across the road in front of the car in flashes of green, turquoise and red.

Liz always marvelled at the tropical beauty of them in this dun coloured countryside. Her thoughts jolted back to the car when the steering wheel under her fingers began to shake violently.

'Oh no,' she moaned, pulling the car over to a shuddering stop, 'We've got a flat. Damn!'

'What will we do?' asked Josie as Liz pulled on the handbrake and threw open the door.

'Do?' said Liz, cursing under her breath, 'We'll change the tyre of course.'

Liz went to the back of the car, wound down the window of the wagon, hauled out the carpet to get at the jack and the spare.

'You'll have to get out, BB. I can't jack it up with you and Josie still in it,' she said drily. BB sighed and got out of the car with Josie. They stood helplessly in the dust beside the road whisking the flies away with their hands.

'Wait,' said BB, and opened the door again to get out her jar of flowers. Liz was overwhelmed with the feeling of having been in this situation so many times before, of coping, while BB and Josie waited. No wonder Harry's mother had picked her as a farmer's wife. She put the carpet on the road and placed the handle in the jack and knelt down to place the jack in position under the front near-side axle.

'Is it difficult?' asked Josie.

Her head under the car, Liz grunted, 'No, not difficult. Just dirty.' When she had the jack in position and had levered the chassis up until the weight was still just on the wheel, Liz applied the spanner to the head of the wheel bolts. Not having the strength in her arms to turn the bolts manually she was jumping on the length of the spanner and getting into a lather of perspiration so she knew she would have stains under her arms all day. She was conscious of BB watching her critically and then just as Liz's weight freed the tightness of the bolt and she moved with relief onto the next one, BB said, 'Is there nothing our Liz can't do?'

The spanner was in Liz's hand and she swung around to face her mother with the spanner raised. Then slowly Liz let her hand drop and it hung heavily against her skirt. It was terribly hot and she was sweating with exertion and her headache, in spite of the aspirins, was pounding in her temples. Her anger and sorrow at Josie's re-entry into her life and her insecurity about Harry all came together in a momentary flash of rage. And the rage was directed at this infuriating, stupid woman, who could pick and prick at her with impunity. As though she had some God-given right to hurt and criticize. But it was not the flash of fear in her mother's eyes which made Liz stop. It was herself. She kicked the rubber tyre with her foot and said, her voice shaking with the effort of control, 'Oh for God's sake, shut up.'

Liz applied the spanner to the other bolts and soon, after further pumping of the jack, she had the tyre off and the spare in place. The sound of her laboured breathing competed with the songs of the birds and the rustle of the faint hot breeze in the trees. At last it was done, the bolts back in place, the tyre stowed again, the car that she hated ready to go.

BB got into the back seat without a word and sat in a huff, her arms folded like chicken wings across her body and her feet tightly grasping the jam jar full of water and roses. Josie fished in her handbag and gave Liz a clean handkerchief which she had sprinkled liberally with a bottle of *4711* eau de Cologne. Liz mopped her face and wiped her hands as best she could.

She turned the key in the ignition and the sweet sound of the car engine sent relief flooding through her. How little it took to make her happy. She eased off the brake and they set out again, leaving the shade of the grove and coming out into the harsh, strong sunlight which flattened and whitened all around them and made the distances shimmer and shake. They half listened to the midday news. It was of no importance to them. In their own separate worlds, bouncing along the back road towards Canberra and Daphne, the three women were silent. The newscast finished and the ABC returned to its programme of Christmas music and the strains of Handel's *Messiah* filled the car. 'Oh thou that tellest good tidings to Zion, get thee up into the high mountain: Oh thou that tellest good tidings to Jerusalem, lift up thy voice with strength; lift it up, be not afraid.'

Liz allowed the music to swell within her and the tension began to leave her face and shoulders. If she could not have studied painting she would have loved to have been a musician, with nothing to explain, only notes of music to express her innermost feelings. If she could have been an instrument herself, she would probably have chosen to be a cello, an elongated violin, with deep notes, resonance.

Listening to the music was good, and she began to feel the way she once felt when she had painted; when the paint from her brushes had lain on the canvas in such a way, hard to describe, but in a way that you could say, Yes, this is good; this stroke is right. And Liz looked out at the dun colours on the back road and saw brown, ochre, red, orange, where before there had been only monotony. With her mind more calm she took a deep breath and began to hum and they drove towards Canberra, shimmering in the midday heat on the plain below them.

· EIGHT ·

On the Friday before Christmas the farm was unusually quiet. Harry and the men had gone into town for the sheep sale. Alex had begged to go with them and Josie had reluctantly relented and allowed him to go too, though she felt a little hurt and left out at Alex's eagerness always to be with Harry. Four huge sheep trucks, the sheep packed in them in layers, had pulled out of the dusty yards early that morning and even the dogs left behind seemed to find it too hot to bark. Josie had wandered disconsolately past them back to the house.

Cynthia was feeling better than she had on the day they picked up Daphne from the airport, and she and Liz were spending the day cooking and putting the house to rights for the weekend. Since Christmas Day was not until Tuesday, Liz had had to freeze the turkey. She was afraid it would go off in the heat. She had asked Mr Doughty, who was 'dating' her mother, to come for a picnic on Saturday. 'Not,' she hastened to add to Josie, 'to be nice to BB, but it might help the poor old codger see the light of day.'

Harry had suggested then that they invite his sister Julie and her husband and their kids over too. So tomorrow was going to be a preview of Christmas and today was a day of preparation.

Everyone seemed so busy that Josie felt she was going around in circles talking to herself. Even BB, whose preoccupation with her new role as Prodigal Daughter Finds Mother,

Returns Her to Bosom of Matriarchal Family, had raised her self-absorption to new heights, was busy. In a burst of activity she had asked Josie to join her and her mother for lunch. Josie had heard her whistling as she put the phone down.

'Isn't there anything I can do?' Josie asked plaintively of her sister's back in the kitchen. Over the last few days they had avoided being alone with each other. And their politeness when others were present allowed the days to go by without resolving anything. On Liz's part, Liz reasoned, it was because she was too busy, and she still hoped that by ignoring the problem it would go away; Josie, on the other hand, having put herself in this position, uprooting herself and endangering not one, but two marriages, couldn't talk about it because she did not know what to say. She had made the first move, but the circumstances of her geography and her character had frozen her initiative.

Liz had wiped her floury hands on her apron with a deep sigh and led Josie to a big cardboard box stored under the staircase cubbyhole. They had to move a few things to get to it, a couple of cases of wine, a fishing rod, Harry's .22 rifle which he used to shoot rabbits, an assortment of wellingtons.

'Here,' said Liz, hauling out the box, 'you can decorate the fireplace in the drawing room if you want to. It always looks such a gaping hole at Christmas.'

Josie had felt like a child being told to run off and play. But she dutifully sat down cross-legged on the patterned Axminster in front of the fireplace and began to unpack the box. Liz's cat, a fat, plush ginger, settled beside her. Ruby came in, but the cat and the dog wanted to play, so Josie got up and put Ruby out the French windows onto the front verandah.

In the box amongst the straw and newspapers were packed the old Italian crèche figures from Josie's childhood. They had belonged to BB's Italian mother, and BB, who had no space to set them up, had given them to Liz. Josie scattered the straw over the hearth and placed the figures amongst it;

the Christ child in the crib, the Virgin, the Magi, the oxen and asses, the adoring shepherds. Lastly, she placed Joseph beside the Virgin, his polychrome eyes staring into some middle distance, at a mystery only he could see. She thought the effect was the best she could do as she surveyed the figures and tickled the cat with her toe.

She liked this room, she thought, as she got up and collected the stray wisps of straw; liked its unexpected mixture of furniture and styles. It was a long narrow room with the French doors at each end, one pair leading out onto the verandah, the other to a small study, not much used in summer because it was on the hot side of the house. On the somewhat ugly pattern of the Axminster carpet (which Harry refused to allow Liz to change, and which Liz groaned would never wear out) stood some of the early oak and yew pieces that Liz had collected over the years; an oval gate-legged table; some jointed stools used as tables beside the chairs; a punched-and-gouged carved box on which stood simple silver candlesticks and a pottery vase with a single branch of bottle-brush. At the far end of the room, flanking the doors to the study, was a handsome pair of Georgian bookcases which had belonged to Harry's father. The whole effect of the room, with its different periods of furniture, with the pale silk curtains on heavy oak poles, the contrast between light and dark, was surprisingly harmonious. On the wall, between the Victorian paintings favoured by Harry's parents, in which the moral sensibility overwhelmed the artistic, hung a small Russell Drysdale of a lone male figure in a red landscape. Liz had urged Harry to buy it one year when the price of wool was high and it was her favourite possession. There was also a pen sketch of Harry by Liz, probably made some years ago. Josie looked at it critically. It was a good likeness of Harry as she had first known him. The long jaw, the angle of his cheekbone, the thick neck; these were drawn boldly. But the lips and the ears, where the curves were tender, were delicately drawn. It was as though the artist had not wanted to reveal this tender side — of herself or the subject, Josie could not guess.

There was another painting by Liz in the room. It was a small oil on hardboard and hung on the opposite wall beside the fireplace. It was unframed and she only recognized it as being one of her sister's because of the little black EB on the bottom. It was almost Japanese in its simplicity. From the date, it was not much later than the portrait, but it seemed to have been painted by a different person. It was a landscape. The strokes were bolder, more urgent than the earlier draw-ing, as though the artist were struggling angrily with the paint. It was a gully, probably somewhere here on Tiddalik, with a waterfall and rocks. Yet the rocks seemed to be imbued with their own energy, as though they took up more space than the canvas allowed, and they seemed to be tearing away from the thickly treed banks of tangled scrub and tea-tree. And in tearing away they revealed, hidden between the rounded thighs of the ravine, a small jagged cave, the source of the white waterfall.

It was a disturbing picture and its energy and vitality were out of keeping with the tranquillity of the room. And it seemed, looking at it, that it too was unfinished, as if Liz had painted it and surprised herself by how much she was revealing and had said, 'Enough' and put down her brushes.

Josie took it off the wall and looked at the back. Liz had entitled it *Birth* in the same elegant, dashed black writing as her signature.

The painting set Josie on edge and her earlier restlessness returned to her. She rehung it and thought that she must get outside, get away from these thick stone walls that seemed to be keeping in more than just heat. She nearly tripped over the cat in her haste to leave the room as she went into the dim hall and took an umbrella for shade from the cast iron stand.

She walked out through the orchard of lemon and orange trees, their small glossy leaves dazzling in the sunlight, but their trunks and fruit stunted from lack of water. She walked under the lime tree, dense and high, near the old tin stables which looked more dilapidated than ever, now that the fire had blackened and blistered its paint. She wondered, under the brown umbrella, how some trees could do so well and some so badly under the same raging sun. She climbed over the split-rail fence and headed up the hill, her mind agitated, while around her the peace and antiquity of the land lay undisturbed. She had read somewhere this country described as the land that waited. The thought sent a shiver through her even though beads of sweat were prickling her forehead. As she came to the steps of BB's verandah, a goanna, sunning itself beside BB's prideful geraniums, hissed and frilled its neck at her before slithering away into the shadows.

'Mother, Mother?' she shouted, 'Are you there?' and with a thin thrill of relief heard, through the spare walls, BB's voice.

BB and Daphne were together in the kitchen, the strains of a tenor voice coming from the radio beside the sink. It was a small room with an electric stove and a refrigerator (still with its baited mousetrap behind), and a square formica-topped table, on which sat a birdcage, pushed against the wall. On one of the chrome and plastic seats around the table sat Daphne, BB's mother.

She was not, as Liz had said on first seeing her at the airport, a very remarkable woman. The only remarkable thing about her, Liz had added, was her obvious, increasing senility.

She was small in height, like BB, but a lot fatter; her shapeless body hidden inside a printed dress with buttons down the front, short sleeves that showed the wobble of her upper arms, and a belt with two buttons across the place where her waist should be. Once, her face had probably been long like BB's but who could tell? And the eyes were milky, but cheery, as though all this thing called life was a great game. Liz had said that now she knew where BB had come from and where they were all going and that what they were looking at was the future, *their* future, Josie's and hers.

'Come in, Josie. Come in,' cried BB. 'You're early, but not to matter.' She pushed the birdcage to one side and flicked at the chair with a tea towel. Bits of bird seed fell to the floor. Josie sat down, the kitchen so hot that she pulled her skirt above her knees and placed her legs so that no two parts of skin could touch each other. She could feel a line of sweat trickling down from the backs of her knees. Her mother and grandmother looked unaffected by the heat.

'Mum and I are just getting to know each other, aren't we dear? And guess what? Marvellous news! John Doughty is going to help her invest her money here. Isn't that grand! Seventeen hundred pounds! Oh it takes the weight off our shoulders I can tell you, and much better to have it invested than sitting in the bank. Putting it into the Building Society, he says he is.'

When BB was excited her voice slithered and darted as though she could not control her tongue. Words ran into each other bumping into the wrong inflection making it even more difficult than usual to understand her meaning. Josie found herself listening to the sound of her mother's voice instead of the sense of the words.

BB was looking remarkably happy and pleased with herself and as if to advertise the fact had picked a dress to wear that morning that was a startling flower print of orange and red. It made Josie feel more hot just to look at it. 'Do you like it?' BB said noticing Josie's glance, 'I'll run one up for you after Christmas when I'm not so busy. Though I did promise Liz I'd make her some crocheted doilies first. I have to dip them in sugar and the humidity – well it attacks the flounces here. If the humidity doesn't get them, the ants come in. Love the stuff, they do.'

Josie had no idea what her mother was talking about but in her present mood and with BB's volubility, it was easier to smile and wipe the sweat from the back of her neck with her handkerchief.

Over the dress of many colours, BB wore an apron that declared in bold letters: Welcome to Mindahra! Sheep Capital of the World! She had bought it, she explained, on a visit to that town with the Lawn Bowling Association when she had represented her local club. And around her head she had tied a paisley patterned bandana. She pushed her spectacles, white with gold splashed frames, further onto her small nose with one buttery finger and smiled at Josie. Josie smiled back.

'Daphne was just telling me about how I came to be. What a book that would make. A film even. I can just see it now with Judy Garland and Montgomery Clift . . . but, you tell it Daphne, go on,' she said jiggling the fleshy part of Daphne's arm, 'Tell me again and Josie hasn't heard it yet. I'll make the gnocchi while you talk.' She was like a child waiting for her favourite story.

'Well, there's not much to tell really.' Daphne's Essex accent was rather soft, and gave her voice a lilt. Daphne also had a little giggle that broke in now and again like an unexpected breath in the middle of a sentence. Josie's ears shifted gear from overdrive to reverse.

'Oh, wait,' said BB, 'let's all have a sherry first. Josie, the glasses are in the drawing room, in the corner china cabinet, and the sherry is here, somewhere.' She ducked her head under the table and began searching among the cartons. Josie went into the drawing room, the curtains pulled against the sun, and found the corner cabinet. Dimly she could see behind its glass doors, BB's best china, cups and saucers and teapots, and Chelsea figures, and trinkets won from fairs, a silver figure that probably was a bowling trophy, some blown glass ornaments and six engraved sherry glasses on stems. She opened the door with the key and took out three of the stemmed glasses and took them back to the kitchen where BB filled them and went on;

'Now, Daphne, Josie's never heard this story before, so go slow. It's part of her story too. It will be like a thread between us, you know? Families always remind me of thread or rope. We are not attached or knotted or anything, but just bits of fibre held together by continuity. You to Me. And Me to Josie.'

Daphne's eyes had glazed over as though she had seen the rope BB spoke about like some tether of a ship that was leaving her behind on a dock.

'Daphne? Daphne?' BB clicked her fingers. 'Sometimes she goes in and out like this. But she's not stupid. She's put me to rights a couple of times. Daphne, are you there?' Daphne's eyes and mind came back to them. She giggled.

'Well, come on then. Tell about how you fell in love with the gardener at the Dowager House and found yourself pregnant.' As she talked BB went back to buttering a baking sheet.

'That's my life, BB. You've got it in a nutshell. A little bit of nooky in nineteen eleven and BANG, there went everything for the next fifty years.'

BB was at the stove beating eggs into a frothy, cheesy mixture in a saucepan.

'You're letting out my real age now, Daphne,' she said. 'Oh, she is a Tartar,' she said to Josie, as though she, BB, was somehow responsible for this entertainment. Which she was, Josie reminded herself, because if BB hadn't decided that she wanted to recognize her mother publicly, and have herself recognized too, Josie would never have met Daphne; this plain little woman, whose indiscreet but fertile encounter fifty years ago had resulted finally in herself.

But Daphne had embarked on the ship at last and was steaming ahead to an island she had recognized.

'You never do forget a lost baby. A baby you have to give

95

up. I was poor but I had a job. My Da' got it for me through the local priest and they took me on at the Dowager house as a scullery maid. They were High Church so my Da' didn't mind. There was a priest's hole in the house and my Da' said they were probably Catholics themselves once and didn't know it. We all used to go up to Scotland to their estate for the shooting season. I got all the dirty jobs. I used to have to take the innards out of the birds. The birds were hung till they were rotten. They stank by the time I got to them. Just don't give me any game to eat BB, I can't stand the stuff, but any Italian food will do me fine.' She laughed and her little false teeth showed prettily in her mouth, and her chins and her arms shook.

'I was just a child myself then really. We used to play games in the kitchen. There was a big fat cook, Mrs Walter, who didn't last very long either. She put her head on the kitchen table once and dared the young son of the Lady to cut it off. Even gave him a big kitchen knife to do it. Little bugger bit his lip for a second and then took a great slice with the knife. I could see the yellow fat at the back of Mrs Walter's neck. She left soon after that. Opened a boarding house in Bournemouth I heard. She could make spun sugar like Rumpelstiltskin had given her the recipe. The whole district talked about it. Except I was the one who had to hold the bleeding wooden spoon handle while she dripped the syrup all over me. We did have fun though.' Daphne went into another spasm of little teeth, arms and chins.

'But, I knew nobody very well. It was awfully lonely away from home. And then – pregnant. The scandal would have killed my parents. In those days you didn't have abortions. And I couldn't have anyway. You had the baby in secret. You hid away from your family and friends.'

'What happened to the gardener?' asked Josie lighting a cigarette and trying to imagine the thin frightened girl inside Daphne. Daphne's eyes blinked.

'I don't know what happened to him. I never heard of or saw him again. It was just an accident. BB was just an accident of time.' She giggled. 'We all are.' She picked up her glass.

'Well, I've been called a lot of things in my day, and some of them not very complimentary, but never an accident before.'

'You're about to have another one,' said Josie getting up and dabbing out a flame that had spurted up from a spill of oil on the stove.

'Don't fash yourself,' said BB ignoring it. She poured a mixture of milky egg, semolina and cheese, fragrantly scented with nutmeg, from the hot pan into the baking sheet. She began patting it down with a spatula but it kept sticking to the blade so she gave up using it and happily patted down the rest with her fingers.

'We have to let this cool a bit,' she said putting the baking sheet in the 'fridge. She sat down with them and opened the sherry bottle with a squeak of the cork and filled their glasses again. 'Cheers!' she said, putting the bottle on the floor. She dipped her finger into her sherry and put it in the cage. The budgie pecked away at her finger.

'Pretty boy. Twwwt.' BB said. 'The best man I ever had, and he *was* a pretty boy, was during the war. He had a little moustache. It was the night the Japanese entered Sydney Harbour in their submarines. I'll never forget it. The danger added a certain piquancy to the situation. Was it like that for you, Daphne? Bombs going off and tracers in the sky?'

Josie looked at her mother with surprise. She had never heard BB talk so openly before and wondered if it was the sherry and the heat. Perhaps BB had altered, had begun to think clearly about what had motivated her life. Perhaps I have changed my attitude towards her too, seeing her for the first time as a woman, not my mother. Josie thought about it and felt the sweat trickling inside her bodice.

Daphne let out a high pitched nervous giggle.

'Oooh, you are naughty BB. I never thought when I gave

you up for adoption that those nice people, that's what the agency said, very nice people, would make you turn out so — so carnal.'

'Like mother, like daughter,' BB said.

Josie began to feel as though she were in a sorority house; a hen house; a sauna; a place in which girls and women tell each other their most intimate thoughts. It was cosy in her mother's kitchen, with the warm smell of milk and cheese, the sound of the bird chirping in its cage, the subdued duet of a Puccini opera percolating around them. And there was the taste of good sherry on their tongues. The hot sun streaming through the window created a languor in the air, in which their feminine scents, Josie's moist eau de Cologne, the muskiness of BB, the dry soap smell of Daphne, all combined to produce an atmosphere conducive to confidences.

'I don't know what it is called,' said Daphne, 'except sin.' Her voice lowered and she leaned forward on the table with her elbows. She had rather fine hands, Josie noticed. 'When I went to him in his little room on top of the stables nothing would have stopped me. He was no mere gardener, he knew so many things about horticulture and the like. He would bring in from the greenhouse the most fantastic flowers I had ever seen. I don't know all the things he used to call them, fancy names they had, but I used to watch him from the scullery door. He would kick off his shoes at the entrance, my Lady was real fussy, and come in in his stocking feet, holes he had in his socks, it made me want to look after him, and he would pad around the house, putting the flowers and the plants in their place, watering the ones that were there. He brought me a peach once; shouldn't have. If Mrs Walter would have caught him, she would have killed him. I'll never forget that peach, all juicy and warm it was from the hothouse. I'd never had one before. He made me eat it while he watched. Didn't trust me, he said, not to give it away. It spilled all down my chin and made a stain on my starched collar.'

All from a peach, thought Josie. All from a peach.

'And he loved carpentry. My Lady said he made the best dovetailed drawers for her dressing table she had ever seen. He could turn a dowel rod into a thing of beauty. It would have made you weep to see what he could do with his hands.' A rising tide of hysterics began to break in Josie's throat but Daphne went on.

'Even that thought, sin, didn't stop me. I was curious. That's all. And it's still so real that feeling I had, of wanting to know what it was like to be loved, that I would have stepped through a furnace if the Lady had put one in my way.'

'Oh, sin,' said BB, dismissing the word and pulling the conversation back to where it rightly belonged, herself. 'One day there won't be any. What would Father Murphy do then? He loves me going into the confessional. It's all about sex, isn't it? And lies are much worse.

'When I married your father, Josie, I thought I could lie and make it work. But it didn't. I was never in love with him and I couldn't make it happen.'

She got up and took the baking sheet from the 'fridge and began cutting circles from the paste with the rim of her upturned sherry glass.

'You know why I didn't love your father? I was engaged to someone else before him.' She stopped with her glass in the air. 'A week before our wedding, my Italian mother told me and my fiancé, that I was adopted. It was the first I knew of it. She had a wonderful sense of timing. His parents called the wedding off. They didn't know what I was, they said.'

'Irish, probably,' said Daphne nodding her head. 'He had red hair and came from Liverpool. You've got his shape eyes, BB. I can't remember much else about him now, except his red hair and the shape of his eyes.'

'I was an unknown quantity. Those were her exact words. "An unknown quantity". They didn't know what ingredients

I was made of.' BB stamped out the last circles as though cutting out pieces of her Italian mother's heart.

'Probably bald by now,' said Daphne musing.

'Oh BB, how awful,' said Josie.

'Well, your father was right there. He always had liked me. And I married him very quickly. Just like you married Michael right after Liz's wedding.'

Her eyes darted at Josie and Josie found herself blushing. BB dribbled melted butter and Parmesan cheese over the gnocchi and put the dish into the oven. She took off her apron and sat down and they all had another drink of sherry.

'Men,' said BB, licking her tongue around the rim of her glass. 'Do you remember when they were engaged, Harry and Liz, and I took Liz to Melbourne to buy her trousseau? Well, I really went there to meet someone.'

'I wondered why you suddenly had to go to Melbourne shopping. You could hardly afford to.' Josie lifted her skirt and flapped it. She was very hot.

'I remember that week,' she went on. 'Harry came to Sydney looking for Liz.' Josie reached for her cigarettes and knocked her glass over.

'Not to worry, love,' said BB, getting the bottle out from under the table. 'Plenty more where it comes from.' She put her hand to the side of her mouth and said in a mock whisper, 'I pinch it from Harry's cellar when they are not looking.'

'You know what happened?'

'When Harry came?'

'Yes.'

'I suspected.'

'Harry came to Sydney. He came to see Liz, some arrangements about the wedding. But you and she had suddenly left for Melbourne on the train. It was May. It was raining. He came to the flat at McMahon's Point. He was wearing a tweed jacket with leather patches on the sleeves. I had a date with Michael that night but I rang him up and broke it. I told him I had a cold. A big lie, huh?'

BB had her elbows on the table, her hands on her bandana.

'I told you lies were the worst. Next to marrying a man with no money, it's the worst thing a woman can do.'

'I really loved him. It just broke my heart that he was marrying Liz.' BB dropped one hand on Josie's. Josie's eyes welled with tears.

'You were so much prettier, too. Like me,' BB hiccuped.

'Anyway, he came to the flat. I put on a blue dress. It was much too thin, so I borrowed your macintosh. We caught the ferry to Circular Quay and went to a Greek restaurant at the Rocks.'

She laughed. 'You know, he seemed much older than me then. I was wondering if people seeing me with him thought I was out with an Older Man.'

Josie remembered it all; a table with a red candle flickering, a pretty girl in a too thin frock, and a young man, he was young too, still in his twenties, their heads almost meeting in the reflection in the rain spattered window. She had wanted him. She was nineteen but she discovered she had guile she never knew she had. It didn't seem to matter to her that this was her sister's man. She could tell from his eyes that he too found her attractive, was flattered by her youthful exuberance, her hanging on his every word.

'And what happened?' BB was leaning forward, there was a small lump of dough like a wart on her cheek. Daphne was leaning back, her head against the wall, having fallen asleep while waiting for lunch.

'We had dinner and we talked.'

We talked and talked. I couldn't take my eyes from his lips. It was as though I had never seen a lip before. Never really looked at it. Do you know his upper lip is fuller than his lower? I wanted to take it in my teeth and pull.

'And after that we went back to the flat. We were terribly silly.'

He was so beautiful, and so unaware of it. That's what really got to me. It was so refreshing after all those boys at dance school who couldn't take their eyes off their own bodies in the mirrors. He had kissed me in the restaurant. He had said, we shouldn't do this. I touched his knee with my fingertips. I'm the one to blame. I'm the seductress. We stumbled to the ferry. It was cold. The rain was sleeting down. On the ferry I remember we sat outside the cabin, because we wanted to be alone, not have people looking at us. The rain was trickling down inside my collar. He was shivering. I couldn't wait to get him inside; to warm him with my legs, my arms, my body.

'And then what happened?'
'He kissed me.'
Abruptly, Josie stood up. Her eyes were very shiny, her cheeks flushed.
'That's all.'
'Oh, hell!' said BB jumping up too. There was smoke coming out of the oven. She pulled out the bubbling gnocchi. The corners were burned black. BB blew on it fiercely and dabbed at it with her apron. Josie began to cry. It was soft, quiet crying of which no-one had to take any notice. The delicious smell of hot cheese woke up Daphne. Daphne and BB tucked their napkins in their necklines, and Josie put hers on her lap after blowing her nose. They ate in silence while the bird chirped.

Except for Daphne, who repeated more than once, like some faulty gramophone record, that 'accidents do happen'. And none of them knew whether she meant their own lives or the burnt circles of dough that BB had so painstakingly put together.

· NINE ·

Josie had drunk too much. She wanted to sleep it off and groped her way into her mother's hot dark sitting room and lay down on the sofa. A clock ticked noisily somewhere in the room. If only she could shut her eyes for a moment and go to sleep before facing the heat outside. She could feel the sun hammering through the gaps in the curtain and waited for the windows to burst. She turned her face into the dark roughness of a Jacquard cushion and willed sleep to come to her.

Josie dreamt that she was back in the dark streaming night on a ferry with Harry beside her. The boat was lurching under them. They clutched each other's wet sleeves. She could feel a wisp of damp hair across her forehead and the coarseness of Harry's jacket against her cheek.

She dreamt that they climbed the stairs of the flat at McMahon's Point and went into BB's room, because they were both so cold and BB's room had a gas fire. She had lit the fire and they had taken off their wet clothes. She dreamt of him standing there while the little white turrets of the fire began to glow red and reflected on their bodies. They had rubbed themselves together like survivors of an avalanche, and she wouldn't release his mouth from hers as though a thousand pounds of snow had in fact compacted around them. They had made love on the counterpane that covered BB's bed, the counterpane that now shrouded the sewing machine. Oh forgive me, he had said. There is nothing to forgive, she had answered. But he knew better. They had fallen asleep wrapped around each other and she dreamt how she had woken up and seen him sitting there fully dressed watching her. He had put on his damp jacket and all the creases had come out. He came over and kissed her eyelids. One and one. His face was white. This never happened he whispered.

Josie dreamt she looked into Harry's eyes and as she did they changed into Michael's. He hadn't wanted her to come, him with his tangled eyebrows and the curls in his hair that kinked tightly above his collar. He loved her, but said, go if you must. It will give us breathing space. Breathing space! There were times she dreamt she wanted to die. Hail Mary Full of Grace . . . Blessed is the Fruit of thy Womb, Jesus. Would the Church never leave her alone?

Josie's mind rose to the surface at the faint sound of a chiming clock. But she didn't want to wake and sank back down and found herself in a church. A church on Lexington Avenue where she was kneeling in a pew and opposite her was a wrought iron gate at the altar of St Joseph and she could see the tools of Joseph's trade, a hammer, a lathe, a chisel. An abandoned apron. No Mary. No baby. And the gate made her sad because it reminded her of Michael and that she was leaving him. And she dreamt that it was her turn to go into the confessional and she stepped past the women kneeling beside her and wondered what their sins were and went inside. And the priest's voice, a beautiful voice, said, 'The Lord be in thy heart, and on thy lips,' but when she went to move her lips, she couldn't, and her tongue had swollen and she was mute.

She was outside, standing in Lexington Avenue in the evening and the red lights of the traffic were heading downtown and the pedestrians walking uptown were swirling around her. And she saw a man, a stranger, and she thought he would do, and she went up to him and her voice came back. She offered herself to him, with her eyes red and wild looking, and he said how much? And she said twelve dollars, one for each of Alex's years. She had followed him to a fleapit hotel on First Avenue. And afterwards in her own bathroom she had scrubbed herself with a nailbrush and she didn't kiss Alex when he came home from Hebrew School. In case she defiled him.

Josie turned her head on the hard cushion but the sun reaching in threw red fireworks in her eyes so she groaned and turned over again.

And in another room, in this house where the walls were very thin, Daphne heard the groan. But she thought it came from herself as she lay like a great beached whale on her small bed.

She thought she was at sea and that her dead husband Porry was with her. But it was only the blue of the walls that had deceived her. Her daughter's walls. Her daughter. After all this time. Porry said, be careful, this one blows hot and cold. That's what Mrs Walter used to say, Porry, that's the best way to pluck a duck. Plunge it into the melted paraffin and then into cold water. Pulls out the pin feathers but it ruins your hands. Daphne dreamt that Porry kissed her hands, red and callused and sore. You were right, she said to his bent over head, she did take me up and dump me. Oh, what does it matter, eh, when we had each other, you and me.

Daphne dreamt of her big fat Persian cat that used to swallow hair balls all the time. She had had to leave him behind when she came to Australia because of the quarantine regulations. But Liz had a cat, Josie had told her. Not one with a pedigree though. Strange isn't it that she likes them and BB doesn't? Jumps a generation. Pedigrees. Daphne's breast rose and fell. She wished her cat was here. Even in her sleep she was aware of being homesick. But she had come, because there was nothing else for her in England. Not after Porry died. BB's letter had been a godsend.

Inside her bulk, Daphne dreamed she was a girl again. She was like a small cargo in a great hull. Oh Porry, she sighed on her next breath out, I told you I was a girl with a past. It's the future I worry about, she heard him say. A smile slipped over Daphne's sleeping face as she dreamt where all that future had gone.

And in the third room of Top House, not dreaming at all, lay the result of Daphne's past, and the future mother of Josie. BB had fallen sound asleep, face down, like a bough across her bed where letters and photographs lay like leaves. BB snored. A telegram fluttered to the floor. The sound of the snore filled the room and the ghosts that jostled to slip under her eyelids backed away.

· TEN ·

It was late afternoon, the most beautiful time of day. Josie walked down the paddocks with the sun throwing shadows like streamers ahead of her. Already she could sense the heartbeat of the days at the farm, and could tell that the men and the trucks had not yet returned. Her dress was crumpled, her face creased from sleeping on her mother's sofa. There was a faint indentation of the velvet pattern on her cheek. She saw a movement under a bush nearby, a struggling rhododendron. Liz had planted it and mulched it but already it had the look of a plant that was going to die, with yellowing curled leaves drooping shade. There was another movement, and Josie hesitated. She heard an animal whimper. It was Ruby. Ruby, sick and shaking, unable to get to her feet. The carcass of a rabbit lay telltale beside her. Josie ran to the house. Liz was sitting in the shade of the verandah reading a book. Liz, come quick, she shouted from the garden as she ran, something terrible has happened to Ruby. Liz put down her book, as Josie panted up. Liz looked at her sister's ashen face and asked only a few questions. Her face was sad. She got up running her hands characteristically down the thighs of her skirt and went indoors banging the flyscreen behind her and went to the cupboard under the stairs. She took out Harry's rifle, the old .22, and shook some bullets into her hand from a blue box on a shelf and slipped them in her pocket.

'You can't,' said Josie. 'You can't shoot the dog!'

'Someone has to. Do you think I want to do it?' Josie trailed her out the door, her body bent over like someone who is ill.

'Can't you call the vet?'

'Oh Josie. Be reasonable. There's nothing he could do. Even if he could get here in time.'

They came to Ruby lying shivering under the bush. The eyes had rolled up so only the whites were showing.

'It's poison. We poison the rabbits to get rid of them.'

Ruby whimpered.

Liz opened the breech of the gun, and slipped in a small brass and lead bullet.

'It's my fault,' said Josie, her hand to her mouth. 'I let Ruby out of the house.'

'It's no-one's fault. If anybody's, it's the men's. They didn't bury the carcass deep enough. Here Ruby. Poor Ruby.' She touched her husband's dog just once on the soft red hair above her nose. She placed the cold barrel between the eyes. 'Don't look,' she said to her sister. She squeezed the trigger firmly. The shot was clean. She rubbed her shoulder and turned away. Josie saw that her sister's face was as white as her own. Her eyes were red rimmed, but she did not cry. But then she seldom did, Josie thought as she sniffed and wiped her own nose with her fingers. Even as a child, Josie found it hard to remember times when she had seen Liz cry.

'I don't know how you do it,' said Josie.

'There are some things that have to be done,' Liz said as they walked back towards the house.

· ELEVEN ·

Cynthia had the weekend off and the Big House lay like an island of silence on Saturday morning while the world around it awoke.

The occupants of the Big House lay asleep while the birds, hundreds and hundreds of them, who lived on the banks of the Murrumbidgee, had begun their chorus long before the sun arose. The birds shattered the stillness of the morning air with their cries; rosellas and cockatoos, galahs and lorikeets, ducks and kites, herons and kestrels. Their calls echoed across the valley, growing in volume as the sun came up, hot and blazing as though it thought it was already noon, until the whole amphitheatre vibrated with their songs. Interspersed with the melodic sounds of the butcherbirds and magpies would come the manic laugh of a kookaburra and now and again the deep boom of one of the bitterns. The occasional bellow of a cow or the loud wheezing of a bull in a nearby paddock was almost drowned out by the bird sounds.

But inside the house, sleep and silence lay like a thin veil of dust over every surface. In Harry's and Liz's bedroom, dominated by the large four-poster bed, only the ticking of a small gold carriage clock on the mantelpiece marked the time. The dark green curtains with their pattern of peach coloured flowers were only half drawn against the light as the windows had been left open to catch the cooler night air. Now the sun, streaming in, burst like a searchlight through the room, picking up the glint of the frame on a watercolour by Heysen, the serrated edge of a leaf on the single rose on Liz's dressing table, the soft gleam on the linen sheet, crumpled over their dreaming forms.

Harry was half-awake. He was tired from the efforts of the day before. More tired at the thought of Ruby's death. He would miss the dog. As usual, Liz had been right. He had seen dogs die agonizing deaths from poison. Ruby had to be shot, and he was glad he had not been there to do it. He'd have a piece of Reilley's ear for this.

He was dreaming; dreaming in that semi-aroused condition in which the mind deceives itself that one is already up and dressed and going about one's business. He was dreaming about his sheep and that he had found an answer to timing their fecundity. He was going to make a lot of money from it, he was dreaming, and he could see the smile on the bank manager's face, the figures in his cheque book, the new fences he would build, the repairs he would at last be able to make. He was smiling, thinking of Professor Robinson in Sydney, imagining them working together on the production of pheromone. This was a product on the facial hair of the ram which somehow triggered the ewes into oestrus. It was enough to encourage a man to grow a beard, smiled Harry in his sleep.

He wished his science background were stronger. It was this aspect of farming that Harry enjoyed. The old days of his father had long since gone. Farming had to be a business now. He thought that if only his father and his brother hadn't died when he was so young, he might have finished his studies, learned more about this side of animal husbandry. But it hadn't happened that way. On his father's death he had been thrust suddenly into a confusion of debts and farm management that he had not been prepared for. His mother, shrewd as she was, knew nothing of running the farm, and it had been for Harry an apprenticeship of trial and error, mostly error, running the property. Mistakes he had made in his innocence only now being put right. Thank God he had had Jim. Jim. The only one who stood by him when he made the painful decision to put off most of the men, to cut back, sell, tighten the old free spending days of his father. Even his mother had been against him on selling off some of the land. But by then she was sick with memories and grief and it had been Jim, listening patiently, not saying much (he hadn't changed) letting him work it out.

When Harry took over the running of Tiddalik, his mother had moved out of this room. 'It's your room now Harry,' she had said against his protests. She had moved into a small room at the end of the hall where she said she could sleep with her back against a wall and not miss the presence of her husband beside her in their massive bed. This was the bed, his mother told him, in which he had been conceived. In which he had been born.

Lying now, in the comfort of long acquaintance, Harry knew every bump in its mattress, every groove in the great oak posts at each corner that rose nearly to the ceiling. He was aware of Liz's arm flung across him, her light breathing, faster than his, the sun streaming in and touching the heavy linen sheets which Harry loved and Liz complained about because they were too hot. But they had belonged to his parents and he insisted that they use them, and so they did, though Liz still grumbled about the laundry involved. He liked this connection with the past. It was his love of the past he knew that gave him the strength to go on. His love for Tiddalik, at times so sorely tested that he could tear his hair out over money worries, only increased with each day he spent here in its house, or out in its fields. He would never leave this piece of earth. He would go on living here even if it became a dust bowl and he and Liz totally impoverished. The very stones of this house had been taken from the land, quarried over on Limestone Paddock, where students still came out from Canberra to camp overnight and pick up stones and fossils. The blocks of this house, with their tiny fossils intact, had been placed here by his great-grandfather, the first Harry George Barton, who lay now up behind the stables under the simple marble obelisk that marked the family vault. The vault where Harry's own parents lay, and where one day, he and Liz would lie together.

Liz stirred in her sleep and Harry opened his eyes. She had tossed the sheet off one leg and the foot lay in the bright sunlight so softly brown and defenceless that he was reminded of a rabbit too startled to move in the crosshair of a rifle sight.

When he had married, it was really his mother's idea. With Billy gone and her husband dead she had turned all her attention to getting Harry settled. She had produced so many girls, daughters of other pastoralists, all of good, sound Presbyterian stock, and he had shown no interest. She had sought out the daughters of friends from Melbourne and Sydney, and asked them down to stay after judicious enquiries into their backgrounds. What schools had they gone to? Clyde and Frensham were top of her list. Could they cook? Were they extravagant? Weekends meant strange young women in the spare room and awkward conversation in the dining room. But Harry didn't take to any of them. And then his sister Julie had introduced him to the Beauchamp girls, Liz and Josie, and his only difficulty had been which one to choose. His mother had tried to dissuade him. They had no background to speak of, they were not from the land, in fact they had no connections whatsoever, and to top it all, they were Catholic. Nothing could be further from appropriate. But he found them amusing and intelligent, and, he had told his mother, they didn't look like horses, as did some of the girls she had produced. So she had reluctantly invited them down for a weekend to look them over. And when Monday came she had told Harry, with pragmatic logic, that he ought to marry Liz. She was practical and not hot-headed like Josie. He wondered still how she had managed to work all this out in one weekend but women's intuition always surprised him.

His mother, like Liz, and his sister Julie to some extent, was always right on human relationships. They had antennae it seemed to him that allowed them to divine what would happen next. He had never had it, never would. Yet for all that, Liz was a no-nonsense woman. He had always been attracted to that. He liked her humour, even though it was often barbed and more than often, directed at himself. She could be ornery and stubborn and cruel with her words. But he saw them as prickles on a porcupine which only frilled when she was angry or afraid. At night, when there were only the two of them, she could be as soft and yielding as the throatlatch of a horse. Velvet. He loved his wife, but he had loved Josie too. That was the crux.

Harry turned over in the giant bed and slipped his hand between his wife's thighs. It was not as though, he went on thinking, the two sisters were alike. In fact they were as different as Tiddalik and New York. If anyone had told him that he would fall in love with two women, two sisters, he would not have believed it. But it had happened. He had always been one for the ladies (not the ones his mother had brought home), but his own kind. There had never been any shortage of women for Harry. He was a physical person. He had, he was ashamed to think of it, been unfaithful sometimes to Liz, on visits to Sydney or Melbourne through the years. But they were encounters, which, while he knew they would hurt her, were of no importance to him. He knew Liz would say that meant he didn't love her. But he did. He could not explain it. And he put it down to a fundamental difference between men and women.

But his real deceit was about Josie. He had met her first. He had been attracted to her immediately. She was very aware of her body, Liz tended to ignore hers. Josie had a way of moving, it was her dancer's training he suspected, that caused her to carry her head in an elegant way on her neck, which moved her thick hair as she walked, swayed her hips imperceptibly. As a partner she danced very well, pressing her full breasts close to him, matching her shorter stride to his. It had made Liz jealous he remembered now as he slipped his hand further between her thighs and rubbed his thumb against her mound.

Ah, Josie. He had been deceitful then. Even now he was continuing the deceit, thinking of her while he touched Liz. The Catholics were right; you can sin in thought, word *and* deed. Liz had told him. It was betrayal of the most intimate kind, not made any less so by the fact that he was the only one who knew of it. He was stroking the silkiness of his wife's inner thigh, comparing it under his roughened farmer's fingers to his remembrance of Josie's skin. The same silkiness, the same opening to his incessant rubbing so that the flesh of the thighs quivered with desire. It had all started out so innocently but somehow the girls had got mixed up in his mind. When they had all first met, their outings had always been in groups, with Julie and with Michael and with his friend, Bob, whom Julie later married. It was never clear in the beginning which sister Harry was interested in, but it didn't matter in those early days. Those were the days of innocence. Friendly and easy. A group of young people having fun. And then things changed, he did not know how, a glance perhaps, a skirt brushing against his leg, and in his youthful dreams, as he was deciding to marry Liz, his fantasies of making love to her and Josie became entwined. The sisters became one and it was Liz's eyes, and Josie's hair, one's breasts, one's limbs, a composite woman, he made love to.

Now as Liz began to respond to his touch, Harry cupped his other hand around her breast, teasing the nipple with his fingers until it stood up and he remembered the first time, the only time, he had taken her sister. How cold and wet and lonely he had been. They had been drawn together that night, left with the city to themselves, the rain teeming down so that he felt they were in some green underwater cavern. He remembered the faint smell of gas in the shabby apartment in which they lived. 'Come up,' she had said as they kissed on the stairs. It could have stopped, then and there. But it didn't. He had followed her up the stairs, hypnotized by her legs, the tapering ankles in the high heeled shoes. When they were inside she had bent down and lit the gas fire. There was no other light in the room. He had found her neck, with the wet hair plastered so finely against it, so vulnerable, that a groan escaped him and he had pulled her up to him, pressing her so firmly against him, holding her head so tightly between his two hands that he thought her neck might break. She had not resisted and clung to him fiercely and they were in danger of falling over. He had put his wet hand under her dress clutching her slim buttocks. She had pulled herself from him for a moment, holding his hands still. 'Harry?' But he stopped her words with his mouth. They had no time for gentleness. They had pulled off each other's clothes, drinking in the first sight of each other's bodies. His hands caressed her belly, cupping the curves of her breasts, stroking and squeezing, while she touched him with equal wonder, the length of his back, the flat triangle before his buttocks jutted out, her fingers, soft, velvety, urgent. And then he had lifted her onto the bed. He had thought for a moment of getting his rubber out of his pocket from his jacket on the floor, but she had fastened her teeth on his lip, she had opened her legs so wide for him that he found himself suddenly within her for the first time; knowing for the first time the sweet tightness of her and he had felt such love and gratitude, such a feeling of coming home that everything had exploded in his mind at once and he had plunged and thrusted and she had gripped onto him as though they were on a raft in a violent storm. And there, then, as he lay spent on Josie's breast, and even now, slipping his fingers deftly over the lips of his wife's labia, rubbing the clitoris with quick worried strokes, he felt a proprietorial right over Josie: because he had been her first. And it was as though he had taken on a duty for ever, a responsibility to her. Deeper than sexuality. Deeper than any taboo he had broken. She had given herself to him just as freely as he had taken her. He was bound to her under this harness that he now knew he would never escape. In his most fantastic dreams Harry thought that the perfect love would be to have both these women, but that could never be. Yet they were bound together for ever and ever in his memory and in his heart.

And now, under his stroking, playing fingers, his wife was awake and responding to him, moving against his probing finger tips, the fire in them communicating to her through her most sensitive nerve endings, and Harry, throwing back the sheet to watch her own and his arousal, felt wonderfully long and hard. At last she put her hand down and touched him, and guided him in urgently to herself, though she hardly needed to, so in tune were they with each other. She put her legs around his waist and opened her eyes and Harry saw the beautiful flecks of green and gold and there was such love for him in them that he squeezed his own eyes shut and held onto her and whispered over, and over again, 'Oh Love. Love. Love.' Until finally he erupted into her and rolled off and sank into a deep blissful sleep where arms and legs without names encircled him, and sucked him deeper and deeper into slumber.

· TWELVE ·

At one o'clock on Saturday, Liz and Josie loaded the white
station wagon with the picnic gear, the folding chairs, the
rugs and the hamper. And a large thermos of ice. Alex, feeling
sore and sorry for himself with a bad sunburn from the day
before, would not stand still that morning to let Josie rub on
some cream. He felt, and told her, that he was not a baby
any longer. It had put her, unreasonably she knew, out of
sorts for the morning as she was only trying to help him. But
he had charged out of his bedroom and waited downstairs
for his uncle to appear.

The logistics of the picnic had been worked out with many
phone calls between Liz and Julie and BB and Mr Doughty.
They were all going to meet at the Picnic Grounds. Harry
and Alex were going to ride there, and Mr Doughty was
going to bring Daphne and BB. Julie and her family would
go directly there from their own farm up the cutting.

The Picnic Ground was a euphemistic name for a piece of
land near the bend of the river where the first homestead had
once stood. It had been a favourite spot of Harry's and Julie's
when they were children. They used to come down here with
Billy and climb the trees and explore along the old splintered
fence posts and amongst the rubble of the chimney stack. Sometimes they would find the handle of a teacup or a bent fork, or
the glass bottom of a bottle, and Julie would want to play house,
and her brothers would tell her what they thought of that. It

was a favourite of Liz's and Harry's too, this area, and in the winter, when the fire hazard was not so great, they would bring a billycan, and some chicken wire for barbecuing and have a chop picnic. It was beautiful then, when the grass was damp and fresh and they could watch the smoke curling up fragrantly into the blue sky. After their meal they would often do some clearing, Liz picking up and throwing branches and bark dropped by the gumtrees onto the huge bonfire they would build, and Harry, getting the chain saw from the back of the truck, would buzz and whine at trunks and limbs to his heart's content. But it was beautiful now too, with the grass burnt white and yellow by the sun. The great old trees, the horse chestnuts and the mulberries, the Judas tree and the cedars, planted long ago by his great-great-grandfather, flourished here on the river bank. But the ancestors, if they had come back, would not have recognized the place.

The site they had picked, while it was beautiful, was found to flood too frequently. It was hard to believe now, seeing how low the level of the river was from the ground on which they stood. The building of a dam downstream by the state government had caused the ebbing and flowing of the river to increase, and here at the bend, where the churning water met the massive walls of limestone, the river gouged out a new bed. Each time they came to picnic, the contours had changed, here a tree would be gone, only its roots sticking out of the water to show where it had once been. And the pump, sucking water from the deep pool, had to be kept moving onto higher and safer ground.

Mr Doughty's blue car had been seen snaking its way slowly up to Top House earlier that morning, and now he too with his cargo of Daphne and BB was heading for the picnic ground. Harry and Alex, having just let the white station wagon through the gate, waited for it to come.

'Good afternoon, good afternoon,' shouted BB sticking her head out of the back seat window. She had a great grin on her face as though the effervescence from the day before was still bubbling in her system. Her mother sat beside Mr Doughty in the front. Daphne had taken a great liking to the man. Mr Doughty, his face as white and porous as bread on its second rising, waved a pale hand. Harry always said he'd never done a hard day's work in his life.

Harry and Alex were just about to turn their horses in behind them, when they spied two small figures on ponies approaching from the front gate. A red Volkswagon followed them like a worried Rhode Island hen.

'Want to come and meet your cousins?'

Harry squeezed his horse with his legs and took off at a gallop. Alex trotted along behind him. The cousins saw them and with whoops of laughter pummelled the sides of their ponies and, slapping their reins from side to side, their white braids streaming out behind them, came thundering up to them.

'Uncle Harry. Uncle Harry.'

They were quite identical, freckled and blonde with a triangle of zinc cream on each of their noses.

'These are the twins, Alex. Margaret and Joy. Commonly known as One and Two.' He identified them with a pointed finger, 'Or is it Two and One?' He reversed his finger and the twins laughed.

'This is your cousin, Alex Rosenbloom. From New York.'

'Hi.'

The girls giggled again looking out of their blue eyes under the tied on brims of their straw hats. Alex had never seen such freckles, so many, so large, they almost joined. Alex blushed.

Julie's car pulled up behind them.

'Hello, hello, hello,' she called out cheerfully. Her husband Bob sat beside her and a large dog took up the whole of the back seat. She pulled on the handbrake and got out of the car. She was a shorter, fatter version of Harry. 'You must be Alex,' she said coming over to meet him and reaching up to shake his hand. 'It is so nice to meet you at last.' She had a very friendly

119

smile and she looked at Alex with an inquisitive, open interest, and then looked at her brother and back at Alex.

'Well, well,' she said.

'Hello little sister,' said Harry, and, nodding towards the car and bending down to peer into the window, 'What's the matter with Bob? Can't he drive?'

'He can't,' she laughed. 'He mangled his fingers in the thresher last week.'

Bob waved a bandaged hand at them, 'It's not bloody funny,' he said, 'I could have lost two digits.'

'And it could have been your whole hand, you fool. Honestly Harry, you know how clumsy he is.'

The twins pranced around impatiently on their ponies and bumped Alex's horse. The horse whinnied and the large slobbering dog in the back seat began to bark.

'Can we go, Mum?'

'Oh yes. Quiet, Brutus. Quiet.'

Harry told her about Ruby. She was properly sympathetic but her eyes were watching her daughters pounding over the paddock.

'I do hope they're careful,' she said. Bob tooted the horn impatiently. 'Oh all right I'm coming,' she laughed up at her brother, 'He's been waiting to see the beauteous Josie for a week.' Bob gave a thumbs-up sign with his good hand from inside the car. Harry closed the gate and then cantered ahead of them to join the others.

They had a wonderful lunch in among the gumtrees on the sparse summer ground cover. They had all flopped around on blankets, though Josie had found it hard to find a place to sit that was not already occupied by a dry cow pat. But no one else seemed to notice them. Julie spent most of her time worrying about her children, telling them not to poke their fingers into holes (in case of spiders), not to sit on logs (in case of snakes), and not to eat the chocolate cake she had brought before they finished their chicken (or they would have a stomachache).

And her children listened to her politely and then, when her attention was withdrawn, went on doing what they were going to do in the first place, pushing their fingers into holes, and under bark and sitting on logs and climbing trees; until she saw them and repeated all her previous warnings. And after the chocolate cake, and the cold curried chicken salad, and grapes and cheese and the white wine for the adults and the orange cordial for the children, the twins both had stomachaches. Julie said she would have to take them up to the Big House to the toilet. (Alex noticed no-one here ever spoke of bathrooms.) There was some altercation about all this. Bob said why couldn't they just use the bloody bush the same as everybody else? (He found it difficult to say a sentence without a curse word in it.) And Julie said they were getting too big to do that, and the twins agreed with their mother and whispered to her that the truth was the leaves scratched them when they wiped their bottoms. And Mr Doughty finally volunteered to drive them both up to the Big House and that was all arranged then and everyone could collapse again onto their rugs or against the trees (which Julie hurriedly checked for bugs) in the hot dappled shade. Alex, his companions gone for the time being, wandered over to the horses.

Julie, lying on her side, resting on one elbow on the plaid rug, spread another biscuit with some cheese, and said to Josie;

'What's it like living in New York? I can't imagine it. Is it as big and frightening as everyone says?'

Josie looked at her friend, still trying to see how the young girl she had gone to dancing school with, had turned into this plump, worrying matron. She was still pretty and her skin had a healthy clear glow about it. Josie looked at Julie's well-fed, bare, brown legs, and looked at her own, long, slim, white ones.

'Well, yes and no,' she said. 'Yes it is big, and no, it's not really frightening. The most difficult thing I find, is trying to find space.'

BB, who had been burbling away all through lunch about her plans for herself and Daphne, and a trip they were going to make up to Sydney, said;

'So many people, I can imagine.'

'That's not really what I mean,' said Josie trying to explain and feeling the afternoon heat pouring down on her, addling her brain. 'It's more the feeling of searching for a quiet space. A space to think without interruption.' They looked at her blankly. 'It's, how can I say it? You are bombarded with so much stimulation in New York you can go crazy trying to deal with it.'

'There are times I would love to be bombarded with anything, except these flies,' said Julie waving off a horde. 'It's the boredom that gets me here. It's so thick at times you could slice it with a knife. And it seems worse in the summer when every day is the same, gritty and hot. And the sky is the same. No clouds. Just heat.'

Josie thought it was futile to try to explain to them the difference of living in a city with millions of people, from living in an empty continent with millions of sheep. Oh let it be, she thought, the heat like pins reaching through her thick hair to her scalp. She glanced at her mother who was leaning back dreaming of, who knew what, stroking her cheeks with the backs of her nails in an upward motion as though she had a beard and was feeling the bristles. Josie looked at Liz. Liz was lying on her back on the rug with Harry sitting beside her, and she began to grope with her hand for the plate of grapes. Harry, seeing this, plucked one for her and rubbed it around her lips before popping it in her mouth. The intimacy of the gesture was not lost on anyone there, except perhaps the recipient herself, who rolled the grape between her teeth and her tongue and said languidly, looking up at the canopy of leaves against the sky;

'Do you remember Josie when we were kids lying in the grass watching the clouds change pattern?'

Josie's voice came out sharper than she intended.

'You were going to be a great artist.'

'And you were going to be a dancer.'

'Me and Julie,' said Josie, raising one of her fine legs and pointing her toes in an impractical high heeled sandal.

BB stopped stroking her cheek and waggled a finger at Josie.

'And you could have been a good one too. A wonderful dancer. You showed great promise, Madame Beryozka said. But you gave it all up when you married. I never did think you'd marry a Jew boy.'

'Oh, BB!' said Josie irritated, feeling the pins of heat turning to sweat in the thicket of her hair.

BB said: 'They did murder Jesus after all.'

Liz turned over on her stomach.

'For God's sake BB, don't start that again.'

'Oh don't worry,' said Josie, 'I'm used to it. The irony is that I'm neither one of yours nor one of theirs. Michael's people call me a *goy*.'

'But you're not Jewish!' said BB.

'Mum, it's a Jewish word for Gentile, that's all,' said Liz in a muffled voice from the blanket.

'Leave it,' said Harry, knowing what was coming, but Liz ignored him.

'And quite honestly I don't see what difference it makes – one way or the other.'

'Oh, you don't do you? You think you know everything,' said BB.

'Oh Jesus,' said Bob.

'Jesus. Exactly,' said BB. 'You can't be a Christian and deny His existence. Either one of us is right, and the other's wrong.'

'The trouble is, I wish I believed you,' said Josie to no-one in particular. Liz lifted her head up from her arms.

'What do you mean?'

123

Josie sat up more straight and ran her fingers through her hair. Her hair felt greasy and her eyes sticky today, she felt bloated and uncomfortable in the heat and she could have been convinced, because of her increasing irritation, that her time of the month was coming around. But there was no-one to tell her to take it easy, not Michael, to raise his eyebrows at her as he sometimes did.

'Oh hell, I don't know,' she said lamely, 'talking about religion these days is like letting off wind in polite company. Everyone pretends not to notice.'

Right on cue, Brutus, lying beside his mistress, let off a loud gastric rumble. They all laughed except Josie.

'Oh get away,' said Julie. 'Get away.'

The dog wagged its tail and inched closer towards her. It was as well-trained as the children. Liz sat up and rubbed the dog under the chin. 'I agree with *you*,' she said. She missed Ruby.

Josie was getting nowhere. She was edgy and dizzied by the heat, by the discussion, by BB's insensitivity, and these things, fanned by Harry's tenderness towards Liz, threatened to burst into flame. She was just about to get up and walk over to join Alex, wandering on his own near the ponies, when Mr Doughty's car returned and the girls tumbled out and ran over to their cousin. So Alex didn't need her either.

Mr Doughty hauled a polyurethane cooler out of the trunk.

'I took the liberty,' he said, 'of bringing down some cold beer.'

'Bloody beaut,' said Bob getting up with some interest, hitching up his pants with his good hand and going to help him.

BB came over to Josie on the blanket and put her hand on her shoulder.

'I do wish you would come with me to Midnight Mass on Christmas Eve and talk to Father Murphy. It would give him such a lift. All this talk about changing things, easing off, it won't do. Why, we won't be able to tell the difference between Catholics and Protestants if they keep going. And then how will St Peter decide?'

'BB, you always get things by the wrong end of the stick,' said Liz. 'That's not what Josie's talking about at all.'

'Yes, she is. Morality. You can't have it without rules.' She thumped her index finger into the plaid rug. 'Just look at Cynthia marching around with that enormous belly. It's not right. I've told you that Liz. As for Jim, I'd have him off the place. But Cynthia, in her condition and with young Alex visiting, and the twins. And them at an impressionable age.'

'Alex knows where babies come from,' said Josie sharply, wondering how the conversation had got so out of hand.

'Well, it just isn't decent.'

'Oh, you're such a hypocrite,' said Liz looking at her mother, and then away again. BB's eyes blazed at her. She was about to reply when the three children came trotting by on their ponies.

'Where are you going?' asked Julie, raising herself into a position of motherly alertness with her neck on a stalk. One of the twins, was it One or Two? called to her that they were going to use the ponies to reach a special mulberry tree where the fruit was too high for them to reach from the ground.

'Well, be careful,' she said, which was the usual litany of farewell on her lips. She relaxed back with a sigh.

'One thing I'm glad of, that it is Cynthia and not me that's having a baby. I couldn't cope with another one.'

'Oh, for God's sake,' said Bob, standing beside the cooler on the ground. 'If you're going to start this women's crap, I'm clearing out of here, for a Foster's and a smoke.'

'Good idea,' said Harry getting up and taking out some cans for them. The women watched the men strolling away, barely able to conceal their relief at being free from them. A ribbon of ribald laughter drifted back with the smoke as they settled at the edge of the river bank.

Julie took her eyes off them and watched her children in the distance climbing on their ponies. Liz noticed and said, sitting up and beginning to pack the food away; 'You worry too much.'

'That's what Bob says. But I can't help it. Did you nurse Alex yourself, Josie? Well, you remember that feeling when you were away from him and it was feeding time and the milk began to flow? Once, when the twins were babies, I got so held up shopping in town, that driving back to the farm, the milk started to come in like a gusher, right through those useless little towelling circles the nurses gave you, right through my dress. Like a fountain it was. Bob said he wished it was beer. But it's the same feeling still. It's like a string that attaches me to them, a little jerk and I can feel it. Sometimes I think I feel more deeply for the kids than I do about Bob. Isn't that terrible? But don't tell Bob. It would probably make him impotent.' She paused and said; 'On second thoughts . . .'

They all laughed, and the object of their gentle derision, seeming to feel their eyes on his back, turned around and waved his bandaged hand at them.

'The father of my children,' said Julie smiling, lifting a jar of chutney to him in a return salute.

'Are you saying,' said BB as though she had never thought about it before, 'that mother love is greater than sexual love?'

'Don't worry, Julie,' said Liz, taking the jar from her and twisting the lid on, 'you'll grow out of it, the mothering instinct I mean. BB did.'

'Now just a minute, Liz,' said BB and was about to go on when Daphne, waking from a long sleep against a tree, called out plaintively for something to drink. BB tutted impatiently.

'Here, I'll take it,' said Liz. She poured some orange cordial into a glass and took it to the old lady.

Daphne was sitting with her stick across her lap and an old cotton gardening hat of BB's pulled low onto her head. She looked for all the world like Charles Laughton in drag.

'Thank you,' she said. A kookaburra began laughing heartily above them and they both looked up but couldn't see it. 'The birds are so different here,' said Daphne taking a sip of orange drink. 'Porry and me used to sit outside the pub in Chigwell near where we lived and listen to the birds. We used to watch the starlings sitting on the electric wires. Like so many question marks they were, Porry said. His mind was like that. We could hear the distant rumble of the trucks on the Overpass.' Daphne paused. The kookaburra had stopped. 'It's so quiet here.'

Liz touched her arm.

'Tell me what you were like when you were young? Just don't tell me you were like BB for heaven's sake.'

Daphne laughed. 'I don't think so. I was me. I wasn't pretty like you or Josie. But I had two men who loved me. One briefly. And one long. I've known pain and happiness. And I learnt that I can live without either.' She picked up some pale leaves, missed the cool green leaves of England. 'It isn't as good living with things incomplete, is it?' She looked up at Liz. 'But it is possible.'

'You are a wise old bird,' said Liz, wondering how many others could see through her. She leaned back against the trunk of the tree. There were little worm lines in the white bark. Daphne took a handkerchief from her pocket and wiped her face.

'Is it going to get much hotter? I don't think I can take much more of this.'

Liz glanced at the sky, 'There's a westerly coming I think. It's going to get worse before it gets any better I'm afraid.' She looked at Daphne, but Daphne had fallen asleep again and she walked softly back to the rug to join the three other women.

Josie's mood had not improved. Even Liz was aware of it. It surprised her. It surprised them all, except BB who never knew well enough to leave alone.

The westerly was indeed on its way. Little gusts of hot wind carried sand and leaves onto the rug. BB was like a gnat irritating Josie. Her voice went on and on, her insensitivity never wavering. She was only dimly aware that she was not getting through to Josie. In the end, Josie snapped – and you could hear the drawbridge going up with a clang.

'BB, I'm not your reincarnation.'

'I never said you were!'

'You imply it all the time. I am not you. I don't like beer. Please don't keep asking me if I want one. I don't like a lot of things you like. I never even wanted to be a dancer as much as you wanted me to be one. I didn't marry the man you wanted me to marry. Liz did.'

'Oh Josie,' said Julie as a way of saying Stop. They were on very dangerous ground. The moat was yawning in front of them. Josie's voice had been steadily rising. She stood up, pulling down her skirt. 'This heat is getting to me. I'm sorry. I need a walk.' She stumbled away from them on her silly shoes. The heels were far too high for a bush picnic. Everything about her, she felt, was wrong today. She set off towards the bank, saw the men sitting there yarning, oblivious to the small drama that had been playing out behind them, and swerved to avoid them. A small flock of sheep pattered away from her as she went down the bank to the water's edge.

She stopped to take off the infernal sandals, and as she bent to unbuckle them, she heard her mother's voice behind her, 'Oh Josie. Josie, wait for me.' Her mother was rushing up behind her. Josie went on undoing her shoes.

'Oh go away, please just go away BB,' she said over her shoulder.

'Now Josie, listen to me. Just because you're upset about something, doesn't mean you have to take it out on me. I'm your friend. We've always been friends. Not like Liz, with her high falutin' ways.'

'Leave Liz out of this. I'm tired of your nitty-picky ways. I can't take it and why should I? You say such cruel things.'

'What cruel things?' BB was standing right behind her. The skirt of her dress was blowing against Josie's shoulder. Josie mimicked her mother's voice, 'You married a Jew boy.'

'Why Josie, I never thought . . .'

Josie stood up, turned around, holding her sandals in her hand.

'You never think, that's your trouble. You just blurt out whatever comes into your head.'

'But how do I know what I think unless I say it?'

'You know nothing. Nothing. You think by keeping some rules written down by some old men a long time ago, you are going to be saved. Well you won't be. It's too late. Inside you are as black as a tree stump. You've never thought of saying no to yourself. Never. BB's always come first with you. Before me. Before Liz. Before Dad.'

'What's your father got to do with this?'

'He had a name, BB. John. My Dad. And you killed him, that's what it's got to do with this. You left us and it broke his heart. It broke mine and Liz's too.' She started to cry. 'You make me pity myself. God I hate you for that. I'm not strong like Liz. You never thought what you were doing to us when you left. All those miserable years, the comings and goings. The men.'

'That's enough.' BB's little lips tightened together. 'And I prayed for forgiveness. I went to confession.'

'I don't care a damn for your confessions. It's just another way for you to listen to your own voice. You have ears BB, but you don't hear. I wrote to you once, I needed you. When Alex was born. You never replied. And again, when I was in hospital, Michael wrote to you.'

'I never got a letter.'

'Yes, you damn well did. But you never came. You never came because you were trying to find Daphne. Didn't you wonder why I wanted you to come? I wanted someone to confide in. They told me I couldn't give Michael any more children. But I never had given him any. You think you have a Jew for a grandson. I wish you did. Alex isn't Michael's son. He's Harry's. He's my sister's husband's boy. And I've been trying to tell you for years. But you never listened.'

BB put her hand out, but Josie withdrew from it as though it were contaminated.

'Don't you touch me,' she said. She turned and ran along the banks slipping on the soft sand, the wind from the westerly blowing her skirts ahead of her.

BB stared after her silently for a moment then shouted so the veins stood out on her neck, 'Try a little denial yourself, you little tart.'

The wind threw a piece of grit in BB's eye and she had to stop shouting to rub it out. The glossy feather from the wing of a magpie caught in her hair and she pulled it off and snapped it in two. She turned on her heel and went back towards the others, buffeting into the wind. The westerly was tossing the surface of the river into whitecaps. The wind bowled her over as she came to the steep bank. She was very small, and she had to claw her way up the side. And when she got over the crest and looked towards the car where the people were packing up the picnic things, she saw Daphne and Mr Doughty sitting with their heads huddled together. Oh how weak that old woman is, she thought, I can't take my eyes off her for a minute. The bubbles from yesterday had finally burst and BB felt as dissipated as flat lemonade. And then she saw Alex near the ponies with his cousins, and a plan began to take shape in her mind. She forgot temporarily about Daphne and thought about Alex. And she rubbed the dirt off her knees and thought what she would do.

· THIRTEEN ·

'I shouldn't say this,' said Julie, wiping dry some forks, 'but I'm going to anyway.'

'Please don't.'

'Someone has to. And I love you and Harry. You have to ask Josie to leave.'

Liz had her hands in the sink. They were washing up the picnic utensils in the kitchen. Liz pulled a plate out of the soapy water and held it for a moment watching the bubbles streak down it before rinsing it in the other sink and putting it in the rack to drain.

'I can't.'

Julie put her hand on her sister-in-law's shoulder. She could feel the tension under her shirt.

'Liz . . .'

'Please stop, Julie. Knowing everybody else knows, doesn't make it easier for me. And although you mean well, your sympathy will just make me burst into tears and I don't dare cry, because if I do, I'll never stop.'

'Liz. I know it hurts, but I don't understand why you can't just ask her to go home? There will be nothing but trouble if she stays. I can feel it. I like Josie but she has no right to be here. And she should never have brought Alex here . . .'

'*Stop it!*' Liz threw the plate she was holding across the room. It hit the far wall of the kitchen and smashed to the floor.

Julie stood silently at the sink watching Liz's face. Liz looked so vulnerable she thought and, what was more heart-rending for Julie was the mask of control that immediately slipped back into place.

Liz calmly got out a dustpan and hand broom from under the sink but her hands were shaking. She swept the pieces up carefully into the pan.

'Let me tell you something,' she said over her shoulder to Julie. 'Harry is my life. He and Tiddalik. We are part of each other. No-one wants her to leave more than I do. But she knows that. And so does Harry. I've thought about it and thought about it. But it's up to them what happens. We're not children playing house. We know the rules. Now we only have to work out which rules are worth keeping.' She stood up and threw the pieces of porcelain in the bin. 'That only gives me eleven plates now,' she said.

They washed the remainder of the dishes in silence to the hum of the generator coming on and off on the verandah. Outside the kitchen window they could see the wind tossing the long sprays of the wisteria that drooped heavily from the eucalyptus. Julie hung up the wet dish towel when she was finished.

'Christmas is going to be a stinker if this weather keeps up,' she said.

'Is there anything I can bring over or make for Christmas dinner?'

'No. I'm all organized.'

'I'll gather up the children then,' she said, as though they were ripe fruits she would pick off the ground into an apron. 'Two's already fallen off her horse and grazed her knee.' She kissed Liz on the cheek, patted her shoulder. She had delivered her warning, just as she had to the children. And she knew, sadly, that probably just as much notice would be taken of her.

'Goodbye dear, see you on Tuesday. Let me know if there's anything I can do.'

· FOURTEEN ·

On Sunday the westerly was still blowing. There was no relief in sight. The walls of the Big House, being stone and built without space between the outer and inner skins, were radiating heat that could be felt to the touch. Liz turned on fans where she could and had pulled the blinds and curtains over the closed windows early that morning. But the dust and grit seeped in at every crack. They had hardly slept last night, she and Harry, avoiding each other's touch in an effort to stay cool. Josie had gone to bed early feeling and looking miserable and Alex had stayed up and played chequers with his uncle until they too had succumbed to the hot sound of the wind battering outside.

The day dragged on with everyone out of sorts. It was too uncomfortable outside and oppressive inside. Josie, escaping the heat of the upstairs bedroom, took her writing pad and pen, and a book she knew she wouldn't read, down to the spare room on the back verandah insisting it was cooler there than in any other part of the house. Harry, who seldom felt the heat, went over to his office at the stable block to work on his charts.

Alex went into the drawing room where he found Liz fixing the Christmas tree. It was a rather spindly pine which looked nothing like the blue spruce and balsam firs that Alex was used to. Liz had a record on, a piece by Verdi, she told him. He asked if he could help but his aunt said 'No, but stay and keep me company if you want,' so he curled up in a wing chair and watched her garlanding the tree. Liz's cat came and jumped purring onto his lap.

'Push her off if she's a nuisance,' said Liz unwinding some tinsel and climbing up the ladder to the top of the tree. The tinsel glittered in the gloom.

'I like cats,' said Alex. 'We have one at home. Cleo. Except we usually call her Puss-Puss. I hope Dad remembers to feed her.'

'I'm sure he will. Michael was always the kind of person to remember things like that.'

'Did you know my Dad very well?'

'We were all good friends. We had a lot of fun together when we were kids in Sydney. Uncle Harry and your Mum and Dad and me and Aunt Julie and Uncle Bob. Your Dad was different from us though.' She paused holding a cardboard star in her hand, one leg on the ground, the other on the steps.

'He was more serious than we were. I suppose nowadays one would say he had more social conscience. He worried about people's rights and things. He was very kind-hearted too. We used to laugh about it because he would collect all the lame ducks around the place and never be able to get rid of them. He brought a boy along once when we all went to a dance. The boy was such a bore. He had terrible halitosis too and none of us would dance with him. Michael spent all night sitting talking with him. He was very angry with us for laughing at the boy.' Liz climbed up the tree and placed the star on top. 'Of course Michael had travelled a lot more than any of us. Me? I've never been out of Australia even. In a way he was more mature. He always wanted to study law and help the underprivileged. But from what your mother says, he's moved away from that a bit. Your grandfather, old Mr Rosenbloom, didn't want him to do law of any kind, he wanted him in the business.'

'Yes. Dad told me that.'

Liz adjusted the star.

'There, how does that look?'

'Nice. We don't have one at home.'

'No?'

'We have *Hanukkah* instead.'

'Ah, the Feast of Light and presents for eight days.'

The things Aunt Liz knew often surprised Alex. He supposed it was because she read so much.

His hand stroked the cat softly as he looked around the room. His aunt was sprinkling fake snow on the tree. It reminded him of the snow that was falling when he and his mother left New York.

His father had driven them to the airport to put them on the plane. It had seemed to Alex, as his father stamped his feet to shake the snow off in the terminal, that he was shrugging off all the words he wanted to say. And couldn't. His father had laughed, catching Alex's eye, saying how lucky he was to be going to Australia for Christmas, leaving the winter ice and snow behind. But he was holding Alex's hand so tightly, in just the same way Alex held his mother's hand when he went for the necessary health shots to come abroad, that Alex knew he was not telling the truth. When his father bent to kiss his mother goodbye, his long dark face with its black eyes bent towards her, Alex had noticed that his mother turned her head so that his father's kiss fell somewhere between her ear and her shoulder. 'We must go or we'll miss the plane,' she said, and they had left his father and walked hurriedly across the terminal. Looking back over his shoulder, Alex had waved at his father standing under the departure board. His father had looked so disconsolate, so sombre, standing there in his black New York coat, holding his hat dripping melted snow beside his leg, that Alex had wanted to run back and hug him. But it would have looked foolish to do so and so he had not. Now, in this hot room, with the warm fur under his fingers, Alex wished he had.

'I expect Dad's a bit lonely,' he whispered into the soft fur as he bent over.

Liz had finished her tree decorating and came down the stepladder and crossed to the telephone on the table near the wall. She dialled and listened for a minute and put the phone down with an exasperated thump.

'That phone is out of order, again. Damn, it only takes a cow to bump against the poles and the wires twist. Do me a favour Alex and take some food up to Cynthia? She made some pies on Friday and she doesn't have a freezer up at her cottage and I know she hasn't been up to shopping for herself. Will you take one up to her?'

He followed his aunt into the kitchen where the warmth from the coke burning Aga hit them like a furnace. The Aga gleamed at them from its position in the old chimney. Uncle Harry had shown him how to riddle the grate in the mornings and pour the coke through the opening in the hob plate. Alex felt quite proud of keeping such a handsome machine functioning. Out of the long low freezer, its generator humming like an aeroplane engine, Liz took a pie and wrapped it in a cloth for Alex to carry. He held the cool circle against his cheek for a minute and then took his hat from the peg near the door.

'Is that you, Alex?' his mother called from the back room.

He went and told her where he was going. She was lying on the old divan, her head on a pillow, her hands motionless on the writing pad on her stomach. She had not written a word past 'Dear Michael'. He could see it in her large handwriting.

'Are you all right, Mom?'

'Yes, dear. I'm just having a quiet think.' She smiled at him. 'You are a good boy. Are you very hot?'

'No. Not really.' Adults amazed him how they just fell apart when the temperature soared. Except Uncle Harry. 'I was watching Aunt Liz decorate the tree.'

'How's it look?'

'Neat. I was thinking about Dad. Do you think he's all right on his own?'

Her eyes blinked for a minute.

'He has Zader and Bubba – he'll go down and stay with them.'

Alex thought of his father visiting his grandparents in their apartment in Florida.

'I'm just missing him, I guess.'

'A bit homesick? Here, give me a kiss before you go.'

She raised her arms up and he bent over and she squeezed him tightly. He struggled to get free, to assert his independence from her. She let him go and he stood up.

'You are growing up, Alex, aren't you? Soon you won't ever want to kiss me. Go on then. Leave your poor old mother alone.'

She grinned and he knew she was mocking herself and that it was really all right for him to leave. So he picked up the pie again and straightened his hat and went out.

He walked up to Cynthia's cottage, up beyond the stables, picking his way carefully along her little path where she had planted pinks and pansies which struggled to survive in the poor soil.

'It's me. Alex,' he shouted, knocking on the door. After a few shuffled seconds, she opened it and he thought how tired she looked, seeing the circles under her eyes and the slow way she moved. She was wearing a long thin dressing gown of faded blue cotton which barely met around her. Her feet were bare.

'Hello,' she said with a genuine smile. 'I'd love some company. I've just been sitting here reading and resting. Come in. Come in, if you don't mind no side.'

'Side?'

She laughed. 'Poshness. You know? Just real casual.'

'Your phone's out of order,' he said shyly, taking off his hat and handing her the pie. 'Aunt Liz sent me with this.'

She took it cheerfully. 'Your aunt's not bad you know. She's got a tongue like a lash sometimes but she doesn't mean harm.' She went into a tiny kitchen and came back almost immediately with two glasses and a bottle of Coca-Cola.

'Have a seat love, and talk to me, it's too bloody hot to think today and old Jim was supposed to come, but I don't know where he's got to. Pubs are closed anyway, and that's a blessing.'

Cynthia poured a drink for both of them. It was a bit warm and there was no ice. She eased herself onto the sofa and elevated her legs on the arm. 'Make yourself comfortable,' she said as Alex sat on a chair beside her. The soles of her feet were black with dirt and as hard looking as horn, Alex noticed. She had very long toes.

'Can I get you a cushion?' said Alex taking one from behind his back on the chair. He was a bit nervous being so close to a very pregnant woman for the first time.

'Oh, thanks love,' she said, lifting up her head so he could push it beneath her neck.

'How old are you?'

'Twelve.'

'D'you like Orstralia?' she said in her slow, flat voice. He realized her voice was a bit like her feet. Broad and flat.

'Oh, yes. Very much. But today I felt I would like to go home. I miss my Dad.'

'Yer. I miss my Dad too. He went on walkabout they told me when I was about your age or younger.'

'Walkabout?'

'Yer. If you ask me, I think he's on the big walkabout. Dead most likely. You're lucky you have yours. He was a real Orstralian, my Dad was. An Aboriginal. His skin was so black, the shadows were navy blue. Can you imagine that? I can't remember him all that well. But I remember his voice, he used to tell me stories. Tribal stories of our people. Here. See that book? Give it to me. I'll read you one.' She flicked through a small book with a green cover. 'The nuns gave this to me when I left. Yeh. Here's a good one. This is about Wuluwait, the Boatman of the Dead.' Cynthia harrumphed in her throat and began to read in a singsong voice probably as the nuns had taught her, but gradually her own words took over and she propped the book against her big stomach and told it to him by heart. 'This is really a story about the Aboriginals of Arnhem Land. That's a big place up north, outback, my Dad's been there. They have lots of rituals for mourning and only when all of them are over are the bones of the dead person put into a log. But you can't put a spirit into a log, see, what the nuns call the soul. No, the spirit gets up, the *Mokoi* we call it, it creeps out of the log and it gets into a canoe made of bark. Now this canoe is in charge of the boatman, Wuluwait and it's his job to row the *Mokoi* to the island of Purelko, the Aboriginal heaven. See, everybody has one, not just the Catholics.'

'Jews don't. At least, most Jews, if you don't count the *Hasidim*. Dad says Jews live by the law, the *Halakah*.'

But Cynthia was imagining she was floating towards Purelko, her eyes half closed, the cool water coming halfway up her sides. 'It's a long, long way, and it takes many days, for Purelko lies far beyond the rising of the sun and the morning star. And there are dolphins splashing along beside the canoe to guide it on its way. And just as the canoe reaches the shore of Purelko, a little bird, a masked plover, which has been watchin' them all the time, rises up into the sky and screeches a warning to tell all the other spirits that the Wuluwait and the *Mokoi* have arrived. And the leader of the spirits comes down to the edge of the water and welcomes the new arrival. Oh it gives me the shivers to think about it, and it tells the *Mokoi* that before he can become part of the life of Purelko, he will have to undergo an ordeal to purify him. And all the other male spirits of Purelko throw their spears into the spirit until his skin becomes hard and nothin' can penetrate it, not even words. No harm. Bit different from life isn't it? And then, the *Mokoi* is renewed. He is beautiful. Inside and out. His temperament is happy and cheerful and he can join the other spirits in Purelko. Where everyone is happy. Universally happy and good. No sadness. No tears.' Cynthia closed the book as though she had been reading. 'My Dad told me once that the Wuluwait was huge and carried an oar and his shadow was so big it could touch you on the shore. I've never liked to get my feet wet ever since.' She let the book slip down to the floor and sat up and sipped her Cola. 'I've got my Dad's eyes they say.'

Alex noticed how deep and brown Cynthia's eyes were.

'My mother was part Irish though,' she said turning her profile again to him, so the broad nose now looked slim, the full lips less so, the straight black lashes tangled at the corner of her eyes.

'Irish,' she sighed. 'The nuns told me. I've inherited her voice they say.' She began to sing softly. 'Oh Mother Mary, Sweet Deevine . . . When the baby comes, I'll sing to it.'

'What colour will the baby be?'

'Me and Jim been wondering the same thing. What colour will it be? I guess we don't care as long as it's healthy. And this is no baby that's going to end in an orphanage or a home.' Her gentle voice was fierce.

Alex sipped the remainder of his drink. He looked at the room, at the poster on the wall advertising sunny Queensland, and a page of a magazine that showed a colour picture of the Queen with some children. Through an open door he could see a small cot placed at the bottom of a bed. A gust of hot air blew in under the door bringing grit and sand with it. He scuffed his feet on the lineoleum floor.

'I hate this weather,' said Cynthia plaintively. 'I wish old Jim was here. He's not a bad old thing. There's good in everybody, the nuns said. He's a good worker when he puts his mind to it. It's just that he doesn't always. Put his mind to it. He and your uncle, though. They understand each other. They got something. They got loyalty. Loyalty to each other. You'se men are lucky. You're like a club. You can't get on with each other, you make rules to get around it. Women. We're not like that. We spend our lives bashing at the door to get in. But the door's always closed. That's what gets to us sometimes.' She turned her head and looked at Alex. 'That's what gets into old BB.'

'Into BB?'

'Yer. See, BB hates not to be the centre of things. And she hates Jim because she's jealous of him.'

'Jealous?' Alex couldn't imagine anyone being jealous of old Jim with his rheumy eyes and gnarled hands. He couldn't imagine even that the same Jim was responsible for Cynthia's swollen belly.

'Yer. Jealous. Because of Harry and Jim. Oh, they go way back. Long before BB came on the scene. Long before your aunt and uncle got married. Jim worked for your Uncle Harry's Dad, see? He and Harry are as close as that.' She held up two long fingers side by side. Alex looked at the square ivory nails.

'It was real sad for Harry when his brother, Billy, died. Jim told me all about it. You see old Mr Barton, he loved Billy. It's not that he didn't love Harry, but he loved Billy more. Parents sometimes can't help having favourites. Anyway, Billy died a hero. He was one of the first in the district to join the AIF and he was sent to Malaya with the Eighth Division. Jim says when they heard that Singapore had fallen and that Billy was dead, the old man took it real bad. Harry ran away and tried to enlist but they wouldn't take him. He was too young. Jim had to take the truck into town and find him. He was on the Highway trying to hitch a ride to Sydney to see if he could join up there. He kept shouting he was going to train at Puckapunyal and then go and kill himself a few Nips. Jim said he had a terrible time getting him to come home. The old man died that year. He never got over Billy's death, Jim said. And Harry had to run the farm.'

Cynthia finished her drink and lay back again. The dark hair around her temples was damp with perspiration.

Alex stood up. 'I still don't see that BB's jealous of Jim though.'

'Ah, you're too young to understand, no offence mind you. But BB has a funny sense of right and wrong. She doesn't like Jim and she doesn't like me. And sometimes I think she doesn't like her own daughters. Well,' she shook her head, 'I shouldn't be talking like this to you. But it is amazin', truly, how she can get things so back arse'ward at times. You'd think she was perfect the way she goes on.'

Alex put on his hat.

'You're off then? Well, thanks for the pie and the chat. And tell your aunt I'll be fine tomorrow though between you, me and the lamppost I think it's going to be a race between this baby and the wedding.'

· FIFTEEN ·

After Alex had gone, Cynthia fell asleep. The heat had overcome her and the thumping of the little heart under her own was a comforting inner metronome. She dreamt of Wuluwait and the dreamtime of her people and of her father and she woke with a start at a knocking sound.

She was unsure what time it was and her body was damp with perspiration and the shadows were falling through the small windows at long intervals. There came again knocking at the door and she heard BB's querulous voice calling her name.

In the three years since Cynthia had been at Tiddalik she had never had a visit from BB. There was after all an unmarked but no less visible barrier between a girl in the kitchen and the mother-in-law of the Boss. Even if the old so-and-so was half crazy, thought Cynthia. And more to the point, Cynthia had the very clear impression that along with Jews, and probably cripples, epileptics and lepers, BB did not like Abos. It was a wonder her daughters had not inherited her bigotry.

Cynthia eased herself over gently and used her arms to push herself up. She walked sleepily to the door in her bare feet, conscious of her crumpled robe and tousled hair. BB was standing politely, expectantly on the doorstep. In her hand she carried an oar from a boat. Her brown eyes, alternatingly equivocal and inquisitive, swept over Cynthia's body and around the room.

'I came to visit, may I come in?'

Cynthia led the way in and sat down again. The thin, dried up woman stood facing her, her feet neatly together, the oar, bigger than she was, upright in her hand. She was wearing a mustard coloured dress, not a good colour for her sallow skin, and a floral apron. In the front pocket of the apron Cynthia could see the neck of a bottle, sticking out like a joey from the pouch of a kangaroo.

'I've been to church and prayed for all us sinners,' said BB.

'BB, what the heck are you doing here?'

'I've come to see you. How are you feeling?'

'As well as to be expected in a hundred degree heat with two extra stone around my middle. What are you doing with that?' She indicated the oar with a nod of her head.

'What? This? Oh. I'm looking for Alex. I heard he was here. I thought we might go out on the river for a while. We can't go very far I know because we'll run out of water. But it would be cooler I thought. He hasn't been on the boat yet, has he? It won't take long to get it out of the garage. Harry's not doing much today. He can help. It would be nice just to have a talk. To get to know my grandson better.'

The late afternoon sun coming through the thin curtains at the windows threw BB's shadow across the room. It looked ten feet tall. The shadow fell across Cynthia's legs. She drew her feet in. She shuddered.

'Anything wrong, Cynthia? You look ill.'

Cynthia passed her hand across her dewy forehead. This is what she got for reading too many fairy stories she thought.

'No. I just got a sudden chill that's all.' BB's shadow moved as she went towards the door. Cynthia rubbed her arms.

'Well, Alex isn't here. He was here, but he left. I thought he went back to the Big House.'

'Well I can't go there. I can't talk to him there, Cynthia. I've had an argument with Josie. Oh it'll blow over but I'm not sure how to handle it. She told me the most amazing thing.'

Cynthia, who had been watching BB's shadow carefully, so she could avoid it, looked up at the change in BB's voice and caught the full blaze of her eyes on her. They sparkled oddly behind her spectacles. 'The most amazing thing,' she went on in that same higher pitch. 'But I can't discuss it. Not yet. But something has to be done. One can't live with that kind of knowledge, can one? I mean, Christ said suffer the little children, didn't he? But I can't take the responsibility of that soul burning in hell. Can I? It's too much.' Her hands twisted the oar in front of her. Cynthia watched it turning. 'What I believe is, you have to make things right. And here is a God-given opportunity to do that. I can't let it pass, not when I think what good I can do. It might be difficult to convince Alex though. But then it is going to be awkward for all of us, isn't it? But it's my duty. I brought Daphne over here. That was my duty wasn't it? I didn't shirk when it really came down to it. Though I do wish she wouldn't suck her gums when she has her teeth out.'

'BB, I don't know what you're talking about.'

'No? Well, so it should be.' She shifted her weight, ready to shoulder the oar.

'I'll just put this back in the garage then. If you see Alex will you tell him I want to talk to him? This really can't wait too long. But don't tell Josie, will you?'

She heaved the oar up and carried it to the door. She turned and narrowed her eyes at Cynthia.

'Have you ever noticed who Alex looks like?'

'Looks like? No. Why, for heaven's sake?'

'Just as well,' BB said triumphantly and went out the door.

Cynthia closed the door with relief. What a weird mood she was in today, staggering around carrying that heavy oar in this heat. Cynthia would never understand her and decided not to even try.

She went into her bathroom and had a long refreshing shower and washed her hair. She put a towel around her head and put on her pink satiny nylon petticoat (the only thing practically she could still fit into), and feeling cooler she went through to her bedroom and knelt down beside the bed. She looked up at the picture of the Sacred Heart above the bed head. 'Oh don't get all over come,' she said, 'I'm not about to say my prayers.' The only furniture besides the bed and the baby's cot was an old chest of drawers which she had bought at a second-hand store and a swivel mirror on top of it which she treasured because it had, supposedly, belonged to her mother. Cynthia, kneeling heavily beside the bed, leant over and pulled out a battered suitcase from underneath it. She pulled it up and placed it on the bed, got to her feet and straightened the small mat on the floor. She opened the suitcase and peeled back the tissue paper which covered her wedding dress. She touched it very gently with her long fingers and then pulled it out to see it shimmer and gleam in the light of the late day sun. It was a heavy creamy satin dress, and against the purple candlewick bedspread its thick clotted whiteness glowed.

Cynthia held it up against herself and angled the mirror to catch her reflection. It had cost her ten weeks' wages; utter extravagance on her part. But worth it, she thought now. She had seen it in the window of Mrs Carmody's shop in the Main Street in town, and she just had to have it. She had paid a deposit and Mrs Carmody had put it away, and each week she had gone in and paid something off on it. And even when the betting in town was that old Jim would do a bunk, and never marry her, and her stomach grew bigger and the sniggering increased, she would catch the school bus on her day off (the only bus that went past the Tiddalik gate), and would go first to Mrs Carmody's shop to pay off her lay'bye and then go to the café for a cappuccino and sit for half an hour and dream about it.

She did hope it still fitted. She would try it on. She thanked God again that it was an Empire line as she struggled into it. She had just got it on and was smoothing the folds over her stomach when she heard a truck pull up at the front. The truck door banged.

'Jim!' she shouted. She rushed at the bedroom door, slamming it shut. He knocked at the front door and she heard it open.

'Are you there, darl'?'

She shouted at him through the closed door; 'Don't you dare come in, Jim Partridge. Don't you dare! It's bad luck.' All the time she was struggling out of the dress, laying it gently but hastily back in its paper and in the cardboard case. Cynthia was panting as she dropped the case to the floor and kicked it under the bed with her foot.

'You're not supposed to see a bride in her wedding dress. It's a bad omen.' Outside the door, Jim straightened up from the keyhole with a grin on his face. 'And what are you doing here anyway?' Cynthia said. 'I thought you'd gone to see the cattle on agistment when you didn't show here. So I thought I'd see you tomorrow. Setting me off like this. It's bad for my condition.' She could hear him laughing on the other side of the door.

'Let me in darl', he said, 'I just want to see you.'

'My foot!' she said disbelievingly, standing in her pink petticoat, her breasts and stomach pushing against the synthetic material. He opened the door an inch and she grabbed the purple cover from the bed and held it in front of her. 'Just a minute. Just a minute.' He pushed open the door and came in and looked at her standing there holding the purple fringed spread around her and looking like a high priestess of fertility. He stood there grinning at her, awkwardly shoving out his thin hips, his thumbs hooked over his belt.

'You're a good-lookin' woman, Cynthia,' he said. 'Bit on the big side though.'

147

'You!' she laughed, throwing a pillow at him.

His voice was gruff. 'Don't know what you want with an old geezer like me.'

'I sometimes wonder that myself.'

He scratched his face for a moment as though he needed a shave.

'Have you been drinking?' she asked suspiciously.

'Oh, only a couple of beers, darl', with some of the blokes after I'd been up the road. I've driven straight through from the agistment, Cyn . . .'

'I can see that. Look at your hands.'

He came towards her, taking his hands out of his belt, glancing sheepishly at his nails.

'Didn't think you'd mind, Cyn. I was missing you. Just wanted to see you.'

'No, Jim,' she said, reading his mind as he came towards her and put his hand on her breast. But she wasn't sure then if she had really said no, or just thought it, because her heart was beating so loudly she could not hear. He put his arms gently but firmly around her, pushing her back on the bed. Half-laughing, half-struggling (almost helpless because of her shape), she said; 'Couldn't it have waited until tomorrow, you big idiot?' But she was now half-on and half-off the bed and his head was buried in her bosom, buried in the big purple bedspread, and she could only hear him say; 'No, it couldn't.' And with a sigh she gave herself up entirely to the warmth of the moment, his need, and hers, as she had before, and as she always would.

Cynthia put her arms around him and the big purple cover spread over him too, till they were both engulfed in it like swimmers in a deep, purple sea. Cynthia sighed more deeply. He had her petticoat off. She was a brown seal on a warm rock. 'Oh well now, my Jim. My Jim. Just a quick one then. And mind how you go.' She turned on her side and he entered her so quickly and emptied himself so fast that even she was

148

surprised. Yet she felt fulfilled and though the word love was never used between them, they would have been too shy to say that to each other, they lay contented, and were aware of it. The light of the day had gone and the palest twilight filled the room. She looked at his hand lying loosely curled over her body, grime in the knuckles and under the nails and she wanted to kiss it. She listened to him breathe. He was not asleep and she felt there had never been such peace in her heart. She wanted to keep it so for ever; her child curled in her belly; his hand curled over her heart. The baby kicked and she lowered Jim's hand to feel it.

'Does it hurt?' he asked.

'No.'

'Are you afraid?'

'Of having the baby? No. And not of getting married either.'

His hand stilled inside hers. He did not say anything. A dog barked outside.

'It will be all right, Jim,' she whispered.

He rolled over and lay on his back. She turned awkwardly and looked at him.

'What is it?'

'Nothin.'

'Yes there is. It's been eatin' at you since you arrived.'

'I'm over half a century old Cyn, and I been eatin' out of tins of baked beans for most of them.'

'Well, not any more, you're not. I'm a good cook.'

He remained silent.

'Jim,' she whispered. 'You are worried. Don't. I don't expect that much. Honest. Hey. I don't need much. Truly. The baby will be enough. And you. That's more than we had as kids, right?'

'The blokes think I'm daft getting hitched at my age.'

'Better late than never. You'll be a good husband Jim. And a good father.' Cynthia paused and said intuitively, 'And

149

about me being an Abo, eh? Hey! Hey! Don't cry, I'm used to that kind of talk. Honest, it don't hurt any more.'

Jim sniffed and wiped his nose on the bedspread.

'Yer. Gee, you're good Cyn. You're worth a bloody truck-load of some of these white sheilas I been with.' She stroked his hand.

'I ain't always been good, Cyn. Harry knows. He and his Dad. I kilt' a man once. I swear it was an accident. He was a right bastard he was. He was a shearer's cook. And there – there was an incident over a sheila. He had it coming to him. I never told anyone this before, Cynthia. But if anyone knows, you should know. In case you change your mind.'

'Is that what's been worrying you? Something that happened a long time ago? Oh Jim. I know you. You're a good man. I can tell. I can tell because you've been good to me. Not many have. Just an Abo, you know. You'll be good with kids.'

'Kids! I thought we'd only have one!'

'Well maybe.' She laughed softly at his expression. You're no match for me, Jim Partridge, she thought. You're as transparent as BB is dense. She grew serious.

'I had a visitor today. Just before you came. BB.'

'Hmmph. What did she want?'

'I don't know. She said she was lookin' for Alex. He was here earlier too.'

'You been busy.'

'Yeh. She was right peculiar. Walking around she was, carrying a boat oar in her hand. It gave me a bit of a turn Jim, I can tell you. I couldn't help thinking of my Dad and the stories he used to tell me. You see, she made this big shadow in the room. And Dad used to tell me about the Wuluwait. He was like a shadow figure. The boatman of the dead. When you die your spirit is placed in a canoe, and the Wuluwait paddles you over to heaven.' Cynthia shivered and put her hand on her stomach. 'I don't want to think about it while I'm – the way I am.'

'You're hedging your bet a bit, aren't you?' said Jim with an upward glance at the Sacred Heart.

'That's not called for, Jim. But she did strike me as peculiar.'

'Did she give you any lip? I'll kill the old buzzard if she does anything to hurt you.'

'Oh Jim. Don't be daft. She's harmless. No. She's just all twisted up in her mind about something. Something she wanted to tell Alex. I think she's going bonkers myself. Know what she said before she went? She asked me who I thought Alex looked like? Now I ask you. What would I know?'

Jim didn't answer but she could see in the dim light that his eyes were open. She shook her head.

'Ah well, thank God, it's none of my business what goes on in that woman's head.'

She sat up in bed feeling wide awake and pulled her petticoat on.

'How about a cup of tea, Jim?'

'Just what I was about to ask.'

Cynthia slipped off the bed and smoothed her petticoat. She hummed to herself as she went into the kitchen. She was thinking she would heat that pie up for supper, it would only take a few minutes, and she left Jim staring at the ceiling, his hands folded behind his head.

Cynthia's talk about BB had opened up all the old wounds. He hated that old bitch. He hadn't told Cynthia everything he knew. He was taciturn by nature, but he knew what fretted him. None of the others did. Not even Harry, who knew more about him than his own mother. You could have knocked him over with a feather when Harry introduced him to his mother-in-law on the day of his wedding. He knew the old bitch as a barmaid from the old days. Of course she looked a bit different, but it was her 'orright. The thought of it made him lean over and spit on the linoleum floor. He'd never have come across her if Harry hadn't been so damn keen on getting into the army. Mr Barton had sent Jim up to Sydney to the Ministry of Labour and National Service to find out what the situation was; he said if Harry was so damn keen to go out and get himself kilt' then he wasn't going to stop him. And it was in a Sydney pub, he couldn't remember which one it was, that he met up with this shearer's cook and BB was flirting with them, leading them on, batting her eyelashes at them. Until this little Italian wog, this runt, who was nuthin', nuthin', came in. And the cook kept teasing Jim about how it was annoying him, to see the barmaid making eyes at the Eyetie until finally Jim and the cook had a punch-up. And then it was over until the shearing season started and who should come in with the gang of shearers but the same bloody cook and the needling started again. But this time, when they inevitably came to blows, the cook fell off the verandah of the shearing shed and cracked his skull. Jesus, how Jim thought about that. He would see again and again, the body sailing over the verandah, the pant legs flapping, and the blood coming out red as meat as the cook's head split open like a coconut. And BB never knew what she had caused to happen. And he never told anyone, because at first there was no reason to, and then there was no way. So he just kept his mouth shut and BB never cottoned on that he knew her once, and he wouldn't take being treated like dirt. He wouldn't take it from anyone. But, by God, he sure wouldn't take it from that bit of skirt.

· SIXTEEN ·

Tiddalik
Monday Dec 24 1962

My Dear Michael.

This is the second letter I have started to you. But this one I intend to finish.

I know it has been difficult for you this last year, and you have been good to me. But I can only keep hurting you. I love Harry. I guess you've always known that. But it's even worse than that. You love Alex, but he is not your son. He is Harry's. I tried so hard to pretend he wasn't. I was thinking of converting, taking the ritual bath. But I can't do it, Michael. He is not a Jew. Here am I, the constant Christian liar, unable to make the Big Lie. To Him. It's a joke isn't it?

I don't know what's going to happen to me. But I'm going to tell Harry today. I'm sick of living a lie. The heat here must be cathartic. I cannot fault you, except that you are not Harry. I'm sorry.

Josie.

Josie stopped for a minute, sucking her pen. She was about to write a postscript, but decided against it. She folded the letter thoughtfully, creasing it deeply and pushed it into its envelope. She got up from the small Victorian writing desk in her room and put the letter in one of its many slots. But then she changed her mind and put it in the pocket of her jodhpurs. She did not want to leave it around. She looked in the mirror as she brushed her hair and tied it back with a ribbon. No more indecision, she told herself. Her face looked back at her. It still looked the same. How odd, she thought, when everything inside her was now so different. She left her room and went downstairs walking quietly on the deep blue carpet. In the stairwell of the lower hall she paused for a moment. She could hear the faint sounds of Cynthia in the kitchen and she saw her sister come in from the back verandah and go into the pantry with a basket and some secateurs in her hand. There was a fresh arrangement of hosta leaves and pink roses on the hall table beside the stairs. Alex had gone out with Reilley, the other hand, to help mark any new born lambs. There were some late ones expected this year. Even on Christmas Eve the farm work never stopped.

Josie went out the front door, closing the screen door softly so it didn't slam. Yesterday's westerly had died down to the occasional hot blast, like the breath from a sleeping giant. She went around the house and avoided the kitchen window because she didn't want to see Liz and she didn't want Liz to see her going to Harry. She passed some prickly cotoneasters that clung to the wall and hid the delicate fossils of tiny molluscs from her eyes. Boronia bushes released their heavy perfume as she passed but she didn't smell them. She saw some small birds fly up from a bottle-brush plant and sit in the branches of a Liquid Amber tree to wait until she had gone.

She wanted to get to Harry. He had said that morning at breakfast that he was going to the shearing shed for the day. He had taken a flask of tea, heavily sweetened, and a packet of sandwiches, two of Vegemite and walnuts, and two of mutton and relish. She had watched Liz make them. Harry said he was moving his small flock of treated ewes, about fifty he said, to check their progress. Josie had mentioned that she might ride over and join Alex sometime through the day, if there was a horse slow enough for her to ride. Liz had gone on stirring her tea, saying nothing. Harry had said he'd leave Trumps ready in the shade.

Josie came to the stable and indeed did find Trumps, his long tail swishing at the flies, standing with his head drooping under the pepper tree near the water tank. The smallest breeze moved the long fronds, creating an illusion of coolness.

There was a tree stump used as a mounting step, and Josie pulled herself up into the saddle. It had been a long time since she had ridden; the last time had been at a farm in the Catskills one summer a few years ago with Michael. But she did not want to think of Michael now. She knew that the shearing sheds lay beyond the bend of the river, a good forty minute's ride away, and were most easily approached by going through the paddocks. She rode slowly over the sparse summer growth of red grass and clover, the pasture poor and dusty beneath the horse's hooves. She was sweating before she got further than the first ramp. She had to dismount two or three times to open gates. Getting on again was the hardest but Trumps stood patiently while she hoisted herself up. The sharp edge of the envelope stuck into her hip.

Josie wanted to tell Harry that Alex was his son. And that she was his too. If he wanted her. Did he want her? He had kissed her that first night she had arrived. It had been a brief kiss but she had felt his teeth beneath his lips. Was that a brotherly kiss? She had to find out. Her future depended on it. There had not been any time alone together. It was not that Harry was avoiding her, she felt sure of that. It was just that the rhythm of the farm had its own momentum. The outdoors separated them during the day, the domesticity of the house gathered them all together at night. She and Harry and Liz and BB were spinning in a circle like the four sides of a dreidel. No-one was getting any closer. No-one was getting further apart. She brushed the flies from her face, watching the steady pace of the ground passing beneath the gelding's head. She felt the heat weighing down on her like a heavy hand.

It had been really stupid of her to antagonize BB. What a mistake. BB had not been near the house since the picnic on Saturday and had only spoken to her once, indirectly through Liz, to ask about Midnight Mass. The last person she should have told about Alex was her mother. She squeezed the horse with her legs and Trumps, picking up the signal, increased his pace. And Liz. What about Liz? Josie could not think straight about Liz in all this. Yesterday, Liz had come into the back room where she was lying down and plugged a fan in for her. Josie had felt like a schoolgirl again, Liz once again looking after her. It made Josie feel uncomfortable; then resentful, which was an easier condition for her to deal with.

Yesterday evening, they had all sat together on the verandah. Josie's first letter to Michael, crumpled, unfinished, in her pocket. Liz had been unfailingly polite. Restrained; even her tongue curbed. It had put Josie's teeth on edge. She had been distant, no, not distant, just calm, calm as always. She was in control of her emotions, her life, her farm, her man. Her feet were on the tiled floor, planted firmly as roots; her hands lying, for once idle, on her lap. It seemed to Josie watching them both that they had seeped into the land and the land had seeped into them. And she wanted to shake them. Because it made her feel superfluous. An outsider. Was she always to be an outsider? Could she never be In?

They had, all three, sat in silence in the early evening, while there was a lull in the wind. Harry's whisky was on the floor beside him where Ruby used to lie. Once, he put his hand down as though expecting to find her soft red head, only to remember she was gone, and he picked up his drink instead. Josie, lighting cigarettes she didn't want to smoke, but finding the silence unnerving, felt a tension building up inside herself that she knew the others didn't sense. And yet just as the sun was going down and she was listening for the answering cry of a kookaburra to a raucous mate, she had looked away from the hills and caught Harry's eyes on her, and knew he had been looking at her for a long time. She had glanced quickly at her sister, but Liz was still looking at the Murrumbidgee, her eyes half closed against the late afternoon glare. Liz was so close to her on the bench against the blue walls of the verandah, that she could see in her sister's iris the changing colour of the sky, the subtle moving shadows of the wisteria, the swoop of birds, the occasional piercing glint of water. She must sit like this every night, thought Josie, not moving, drinking it in, this air of Tiddalik, her hands limp in her lap, the fingers curled upwards, the palms exposed. Liz had no tensions, why should she? It was only in herself, Josie thought, that tension was coiled like a steel spring. Sometimes this spring seemed so tightly coiled it felt as dense as a steel bearing and yet it burned. Josie felt as she had on Saturday, that she was in danger of bursting into flame. And it had only been the heat, and her mother, that had caused her outburst then, not her body, that she had been so quick to blame.

They had eaten a cold meal from a trolley on the verandah, and had washed up silently, each of them still in a dream-like state. Alex had joined them for supper and then gone back to his room, to finish wrapping presents and listen to the radio. The telephone bell had jarred them from the ticking silence. It was BB, Liz said, asking if Josie still wanted to go to Midnight Mass on Christmas Eve, or if she should get Mr Doughty to take her and Daphne? She didn't want to ask Mr Doughty, she said, because she thought he was up to something. Josie had hesitated. She really didn't want to be with BB. But Daphne would be there and, well, it was a good way of getting over this silly awkwardness. When Liz had hung up the phone, she asked Liz if she would come too? Liz said, no, she had stopped going long ago.

Josie had come to the end of her long ride and saw ahead of her the crude buildings that comprised the shearing sheds. The main building was of corrugated iron with ramps and sheep pens tacked onto it. Behind and slightly to one side, was a long low building of mud-bricks which were the shearers' quarters. All was quiet and empty now except for Harry's horse, Polo, tied to a post in the shade nearby, its saddle over the rail. Josie slid off Trumps and hooked the bridle back to the saddle and tied the horse with a rope halter to the same post.

She climbed the steps to the shearing shed and it took some minutes for her eyes to adjust to the dimness after the glare of the bright sunlight. The sweet-sour smell of sheeps' wool and old droppings filled her nostrils. She crossed the grated wood floor, passed the empty shearers' stands and the silent chutes where the sheep were pushed down to the pens below. Beyond the wool classer's table, she could see Harry in a penned off area bending over his sheep. Above the bleating of the sheep he did not hear her footsteps. He was absorbed in his work and she sat on a low rail watching him, the sun raking him through the dusty broken windows, through the spaces between the roof and the walls. He was suddenly aware of her presence and turned and straightened up. He pushed his hat back off his forehead. His face was beaded with sweat; his shirt, the sleeves rolled up, sticking to him in dark patches. The hair on his arms was matted and dusty. His hands however were remarkably clean.

'Well, hello,' he said. 'What are you doing here?'
'I felt like the ride.'
'I thought you were going to catch up with Alex?'
'I . . . I changed my mind.'
She came off the rail towards him. 'Can I help?'

'Sure. Jim hasn't turned up, the old bastard. Liz may be right about him.' He picked up a sheaf of papers on a clipboard.

'Look. You can check off the numbers. Here.' He pointed to columns evenly drawn on the sheets. He told her these were his charts for controlled breeding. There were many different pages, all filled neatly with Harry's handwriting. One sheet was headed *Ewe Data Sheets*. Under that, other headings, *Sponge In/Out, Date Raddled, Date Lambed, Lambs*. Under that, other sub-headings, *In/Out, Control Cycle, 2nd Cycle, Lambs Born, Marked* and *Weaned*. On another sheet, *Ages of Ewes, 2 Tooth, 4 Tooth, 6 Tooth, Full Mouth*. There were columns for *Dates of Shearing, Dipping, Crutching, Lambing, Weaning*. On the last sheet, entries for *Date of Sponge Insertion, Sponge Removal, Numbers of Sponges Expelled*.

'See here,' he was saying, 'just put a tick in the column I tell you, OK? I'm nearly finished anyway. I'll give you the number of each sheep from the tag in its ear.'

'I never knew it was so scientific,' she said with a laugh. 'I just thought you left them all out in the paddocks to get on with it.'

'That was in the good old days,' he said with a smile. 'And we are not really so scientific, though we try to be.'

He paused for a minute and gave her a wicked grin, 'You sure you want to watch this?'

'Of course,' she said.

She settled again on the rail watching him, watching his sure, deft way with animals. A quick grasp, holding them firmly while they struggled, reading the number on the red tags on their ears, turning them around, holding them with his knees, removing a synthetic tampon from the uterus.

'What is that?' she giggled.

He was dipping his hand in a bucket of disinfectant, picking up a syringe. He talked as he worked.

'My experiment. These are maiden ewes. I'm withdrawing these sponges because I hope they've done the trick.'

'What trick? What are they?'

'They are a progestogen device. It brings the ewes into oestrus.' He turned and smiled at her releasing one sheep and grabbing another. 'Into heat that is for you city people.'

He went back to his work. 'If the sponge is still here, I remove it and inject them.' He called a number to her and she ticked it in the appropriate column.

'What do you inject them with?'

He plunged the needle neatly into the sheep before answering.

'Well, it's a serum, really. The local vet gets it for me. From pregnant mares.' The sheep he was holding bleated furiously and fought and then scrambled free as he pushed it through the gate behind him into another pen. The pen led to a chute and the sheep joined its companions in the yard below. Josie could see them milling about under her feet through the grated floor. Harry caught another sheep and called out its number. He probed for the sponge but there was none. He put the sheep in a different pen from the others. He grabbed another, removed the sponge, injected it and sent it on its way. When they were all through, Harry washed off his hands and arms from a tap in the corner and splashed his face and hair. He came over to her wiping his face and hands on a towel he had taken from a nail in the corner post.

'You're a good partner, Josie.'

'Thanks. Here.' She handed him the charts and he looked over them making one or two notations of his own. The mob of sheep below them sent up pungent drafts of dust.

'And the ewes,' she said, 'what happens to them now?'

'Well this one has to wait till my next lot go through,' he said, indicating the one forlorn sheep in the upper pen. He led the way down the ramp of the chute, doubling over in the small space. He gave her his hand to steady her as she ran down behind him. He raised his voice over the babbling noise of the animals.

'These will mate the day after tomorrow. I've got six healthy rams waiting for them.' They walked through the flock, the soft bodies bumping against their legs. Harry led the way to the verandah of the shearers' quarters. His saddle-bag lay on the wooden floor.

'It all looks so desolate now,' he said. 'You can't imagine what it's like when the gang of shearers is here, and their cook and the rouseabouts. The noise! The arguments! But it's a lot of fun in spite of the hard work.' He put his hands flat on the raised verandah floor and hoisted himself up onto the edge. Josie walked up the steps and came and sat beside him. He poured some tea into the lid of the flask and offered it to her, and took his cigarettes out of his buttoned shirt pocket.

'Ah, it's fine here, then,' he said lighting his cigarette and then lighting one for her. He took it from his mouth and gave it to her.

'I hope these results are better,' he said, watching his sheep with his farmer's eye. 'Last year I lost a lot. Too many. We were trying implants then. Under the skin. Too damn difficult. But this seems better. We're on to something that's for sure. We can lamb regularly. And when we want to, if it's done right. It's just a matter of good husbandry. Think what it would mean to the sheep industry in this country. More lambs. More food.' He smiled. 'More money to pay off my overdraft.' He laughed, and drew contentedly at his cigarette, holding it between his thumb and first finger, his palm open to her.

'You love this, don't you? All this, I mean? The sheep, the outdoors, the heat.' She swatted at a persistent fly trying to land in her tea.

'I suppose I do.'

She looked at him, his face in profile, turned away from her, looking at his sheep and his farm, his eyes squinting from the sun and the smoke from his cigarette. Her heart made a leap inside her so tangible that she caught her breath. His profile was clean, chiselled. The nose, the surprisingly full lips, the square chin, all seemed outlined with a dark pencil against the plaster wall of the building. It seemed as though he was being seared into her memory and that if ever she shut her eyes, he would be there, his profile, a negative imprint on her retina. Josie struggled with her emotions. I love him, she thought. But he seemed oblivious to her, unaware of what she was thinking, of what track her thoughts were following and had been on for so long.

'Just as well too I reckon,' he went on. 'Since it's all I've got. Acres and acres of dust. Years of work. And I owe more money now than I did when I began.' He did not sound bitter. He turned to her. His gold eyes dazzled her. She looked away, poured out the dregs of her tea onto the earth below her dangling feet. She poured some for him. When he took it their fingers touched. He sipped the tea watching her. She moved her arms so that she was leaning back on her elbows. His eyes moved over her. She was very conscious of having his attention. She held his eyes for a moment and then looked away at the flock of sheep they had just left.

'There's so much that's cruel, isn't there?'

'In farming?'

'Yes. In farming. What you do to the ewes. And the rams.'

'Just as well you haven't watched us castrate the male lambs. We bite those little fellow's balls out with our teeth.' He was laughing at her softly.

'Oh, Harry,' she said.

'It's true. And once upon a time, I read it somewhere in one of Dad's books, the male lambs were castrated by merely twisting the testicles round in the scrotum until they became like a rope and just withered away.'

He laughed again, sure of his own masculinity.

'It's all so premeditated,' she said. 'No chance encounters.

Everything worked out. The timing. The matings. It's like you're playing God.'

She broke off a splinter from the planking of the verandah floor and went on: 'If their cycle doesn't fit, why, you can change the cycle. If they have one lamb, you can inject them and they can have twins. If they have two, then why not have triplets? It's all so easy. All so artificial. Do you think they know?'

He laughed. 'They're only sheep, Josie. And it's not all that foolproof yet. Besides, half the injections I give them are for their health. I worry more about them than I do about myself.'

'What I was getting at was the seeming predestination of it all. I wonder whether we're like sheep too.' She paused.

'I don't know. I don't think about it, I guess. I'm too busy getting through the day.'

'I remember you once saying how we must all grasp at good fortune – chance – when it comes. Do you remember that? I've never forgotten. It was the first time you kissed me.'

'Machiavelli. Fortuna. But I was younger then. Didn't know what responsibilities were. Choices were very simple then.'

'I never made any. Choices.'

'Since when did you become such a fatalist?'

'Since I fell in love with you.'

'Oh Josie.' His voice had a finality about it.

'Harry,' she said pulling her legs up and kneeling beside him. 'It's true. Ever since I first saw you. When I met you in Sydney and we used to come down with Julie to visit. And the one night we had. Remember how it rained? I loved you Harry.' He was very quiet. Josie went on, her voice soft, urgent.

'And you know something I've never understood? If I had been older, I would have fought for you. I would have grasped at my chance. But I didn't. I pulled back. Oh God, if I could turn back the clock, I would fight for you. But you, why didn't you fight? Why didn't you change your mind about Liz? Yes, it would have been difficult and awkward. But we could have worked something out. Harry, you loved me then, didn't you? I know you loved me that night in Sydney. You couldn't have pretended.'

He was silent. Only the bleating of the sheep and the cries of the curlews answered her.

'God damn you! That night. It happened! Did you, did you love me then?'

He put out his cigarette in the remains of the tea in the lid, grinding the butt deliberately into fragments.

'I think we ought to go.' He jumped down from the verandah onto the earth. He reached for the flask beside her. She put her hand over his.

'Please don't cut me off. We have to talk about it. Why can't you talk about it?' Her eyes filled with tears. She fought it. She was ashamed and infuriated at her own weakness.

But the tears softened him.

'There are some things Josie that are best left unsaid and buried.'

'But what if things can't be buried? What if they are growing? You said yourself we could change things.'

He groaned. 'You twist words.'

She jumped down beside him, her fingers clenched at her side.

'Change things,' she said.

He turned abruptly away from her, his back stiff with anger.

'I can't Josie. For God's sake. I can't!'

She placed her hand on his elbow. It was as though she had touched a detonator. He shouted out; 'Liz! Liz!' Liz. Liz. Liz. His voice echoed around the hills. The cries of the sheep filled the silence. The horses whinnied on the other side of the shearing shed. Harry spun round, his eyes angry, his face distorted. She could see his head outlined against the sky. He gripped her arms so fiercely that she winced.

'You want the truth, Josie? Only the truth? I'll give you the truth. Yes. I loved you. God, if I die in hell. I loved you. And I still love you. But some things cannot be. Don't you understand that? Does it make it any easier to accept that? By knowing the truth? Does it?' He shook her. 'Oh Jesus Christ Almighty.'

'I love you Harry,' she said.

He did not answer but let go her arms so that the blood rushed into her hands again. He stood looking at her for a long moment and then he took her face, just as fiercely as he had held her arms, and kissed her, her mouth, her eyelids, her cheeks, the corners of her lips. She tried to kiss him back, but he had bent his head, was kissing her throat, her ear, her chin. Josie flung her arms around him. He lifted her up as easily as if she weighed no more than one of his sheep. He climbed the four steps onto the verandah and kicked open the door. She was vaguely aware of a kitchen and a corridor and then another door where an open pallet on a small poor bedstead remained from the last shearing season. He threw her on it unceremoniously, slammed the door with his foot.

He came to her, pulling off his shirt, his eyes on hers, his expression one of anger. He pulled the band from her hair. He opened her blouse undoing the buttons with light, quick fingers. His hands were on her breasts freeing them from her blouse. His face, his chin, rubbed against her nipples, her swelling breasts snowy against his sunburnt face. She took his head up with her hands and placed her lips very carefully and deliberately on his, sucking him as though he were a flower, or a piece of fruit and she was trying to draw up all his goodness through her mouth. Her nostrils were full of his male smell. His skin was beautifully smooth, finely pored as she remembered. He knelt over to pull off her boots and then her jodhpurs. She writhed to help him. She was under him, she stroked him, she touched the hair under his arms. He did not stop to take off his boots or moleskins. He was unbuttoned and in her before she knew it. They were pulsating together, her hands exploring the powerful muscles of his body, feeling them contracting as he rose and fell on top of her. Their movement caused dust to rise from the ticked pallet and as they exploded and came to orgasm together, the dust motes in the sunlight seemed in Josie's eyes to have turned to stars. For a minute she thought that day had turned to night. He rolled off and Josie bent to take off his boots and trousers. She touched him until he was aroused and then she straddled him as if he were a horse and she the rider. Her hair, flowing free, free of its ribbon, brushing against his face. Her breasts, swinging above him, tantalizing him so that he arched to kiss her, bite her, suck her, and she would arch back so that now he had her, now he did not, and all the time, the rhythmic movement of her hips did not alter. Forward and back on him, side to side, like a horse on a carousel except now she was impaled on the pole. Was she the horse, was she the rider? Her every nerve end was glutted with satisfaction. They were slipping and sliding on each other, up and down. His hands, her hands, his chest, her breasts, his face, her mouth, his buttocks, her hips. They were lost until he said, 'Now. Now.' And it was time. He bit her left breast with his teeth and they were bucking and rolling with each other, his arms no longer wandering over her, but holding her firmly, one on each side of her hips, until he was pounding into her and she could not shake him loose and she cried out, 'Harry, Harry. At last, at last.'

· SEVENTEEN ·

But they were not finished.

He said to her quietly, his lips in the hollow between her collarbone and her throat; 'I will never leave Liz. There is nothing you can do or say that will change that.' He kissed her mole.

She opened her lips to protest, but he laid one finger on them. He had done that to her before. She looked into the tawny eyes, seeing the flecks of gold in them, like splinters of the sun, and tried to fathom his meaning. Her mind was unable to accept that he meant what he said. And there in the pupil she saw her reflection miniaturized, pale; but clear enough, detailed enough, to see her own expression, incomplete, desirous, a bud that would never open. And in a flash Josie saw her life ahead, just like this, something pale and spreadeagled, always on the verge of satisfaction, tantalized but never realized. The vision was so acute, so despairing that she sobbed, 'Oh Harry. Please. Please.' And she did not know what she asked for.

'Tell me again you love me,' he said. He was playing with her, licking his rough tongue around her throat, her ears.

'I love you Harry. I love you more than I love myself.'

He kissed her gently on the mouth, took his mouth from hers a moment to utter, 'Liar', and before she could respond he was kissing her again, plunging his tongue into her mouth, their bodies again united, so deeply, so deliciously that Josie felt she was only a vessel being filled at two ends, yet conversely, and at the same time, that she wanted to be him, to be a man, to intrude into him, to have power over him: to see everything clearly and coldly without the bother of thinking like a woman. And then the thought was gone and she was again transported out of herself and all her dreams and fantasies, her very existence and identity, were wrapped up in this one glowing being that she held, held, held, because this, this was the only time she could have him to herself. They were spent. And she could swear it was night again except the blackness gradually ebbed away, the sun felt hot on her body and she could hear birds and sheep outside and the faint, distant sounds of cattle bellowing. She kissed his fingers. She could smell herself on him. She kissed them again. He got up without a word and pulled on his moleskins.

He looked at her, pushed back the hair from her temple.

'I'll get some water,' he said.

Josie listened to him splashing water in the kitchen. She looked around this bare room, the cracked, peeling plaster, the hot sun falling barred across the mattress she lay on, making a cross on her white body. She looked at the ceiling where a light bulb hung listlessly on a cord. She suddenly felt very naked; smooth, forlorn and cold like the light bulb. She sat up and put on her clothes before Harry came back. She joined him in the kitchen and washed her face and pulled his comb through her hair.

Harry and Josie went outside. The heat slapped them in the face. They did not touch each other until he saddled her horse and helped her onto it. He stood holding her booted foot.

'You are very beautiful Josephine Rosenbloom. Rose in bloom.' He drew a heart with his finger on the dust on her boot.

'I came here Harry for you. Me and Alex.'

'Ah. Are you sure of that Josie? You came for me? Not

for you? Wouldn't you have stayed away if that were true?'

A needle touched her heart. A feeling of dread. She shrugged it off.

'We can work it out.'

He was still holding her foot, caressing her ankle where the top of her boot met the cuff of her jodhpurs.

'How my beauty? Do you think anything has really changed? Because I've given in? Do you think I would leave Liz, our twelve years together, what we've been through, for you? How little you understand love.' He was talking so gently, as though she were a child with a terminal illness. 'Once,' he said, 'I might have been able to throw it all away. For you. But not now. I can't live without Liz, Josie. We've been through a lot together. Disappointments. She knows me. Knows me, Josie, and still loves me. How could I leave her after that?'

He wiped the dust off her boot with his hand. He said very quietly, 'You've only made it worse coming here. Harder to accept. Do you think it's been easy for me, having you in the same house, knowing you were sleeping one wall away from me?'

'Harry.'

He had swung his own saddle onto his horse, was buckling the saddlebag back on. He put his foot in the stirrup and swung up easily. His eyes were level with hers. He pulled his hat down more firmly so they were shaded from the sun. She couldn't see their expression.

'I never wanted this to happen, Josie. I swear. I do love you Josie, but I love her too. You must leave us alone Josie. You don't belong here.'

'No!'

Her horse started at the violent jerking of its reins. Harry leaned over and grabbed them.

'Josie. I don't mean to hurt you. For God's sake listen! You seem to think you are the only one capable of caring.

169

That night in Sydney; I knew Liz would be away. I came to see you, to try to sort out my own feelings. But it all got more entangled. I didn't want to hurt you. I didn't want to hurt her. I did the easiest thing. The weakest thing. I left everything the way it was. Why couldn't you?'

'Because something happened.' Oh Alex, Alex. Should I tell him now about Alex?

'You and Michael. Go home to Michael. You have love there.'

'Not like this.'

'There are different types of love, Josie. You know that. And some are more binding than others. I am bound to Liz and she to me. You are bound to Michael and Alex.'

'You sanctimonious pig.' She said it quietly but she knew she had cut him because the veins on his hands stood out where they still grasped her reins.

The wind whipped up and his hat fell off and he caught it halfway but she could see his eyes. He gave her a long hard look. It was a look she never wanted to see on his face again.

'Did you really think that love was free of risk?'

He made a curious gesture with his hat, as though tipping it like some old-fashioned gentleman. It was so incongruous that if Josie had not been so miserable, so angry, she would have laughed.

He reined his horse around. 'I'm going over to see the pump. Will you be all right?' It was a polite stranger asking.

She couldn't lift her eyes to him. Couldn't bear to see this stranger whose body she felt still inhabited hers, whose face she would see each time she looked at her son.

'I'll see you back at the house, then.'

She lifted her eyes when it was safe to do so, watching him ride away, sitting easy in his saddle. The brown hills around her seemed to swim in a haze as though her whole world was being tilted. When the horizon swung back into steady view and she looked again to see him, he was gone.

She had never felt so utterly alone, with such pain in her heart that breathing was difficult. Her heart and her body had become one. Even those years ago when she had suspected she was pregnant and Liz and Harry got married, she had not felt so isolated. The hurt then was salved with hope; the hurt now, with desolation. She threw her arms now onto the one, warm, living thing near her and sobbed into the horse's mane.

A long, raw, unnerving time later, she set the horse in motion and headed across the river flats. She had no idea how long it took her to get there. She would stop at gaunt trees and stare at their silhouettes, seeing in them arms beseeching water from the sky. A lone hawk rose up at her approach and circled her endlessly. She crossed the flats, which, when the river was high were completely under water, but now retained only the dried, cracked hoof prints of cattle and sheep long gone to slaughter. Over the pebbles of a dried up tributary, the dead bed of Mountain Creek, her horse's hooves clink-chinked. Once, Trumps slipped, the smooth, shiny pebbles, perfect but treacherous underfoot. Leaves blew across their path. How crispy they sounded as they tapped against them. She stopped to open a gate and her eyes were riveted by the weathered appearance of the posts, mountain ranges of peaks produced in miniature. Oh, she thought, how wintry this place is in the height of its summer.

She could not go on. It was the heat sapping her. That was all. She knew now how these trees survived, how they gave up their colour to the sun; said, yes, yes, take me, take my green, my water, my beauty, just let me live. And did; their lives – their leaves – drooping. She dismounted. She sat on the earth holding the docile, exhausted horse by the rein. She plucked at the grass. A few upright blades in the parched, cracked earth. The surface of the earth was glossy smooth, the mud having left behind the reflected memory of its water. But she could scrape it with a fingernail, and underneath was revealed, dust: dust crumbling into nothingness between her fingers. A pale mauve flower. The scent of wisteria. How long ago had it been since she had felt that silken little petal, bruised it between her fingers, felt how damp it was? An eternity. There were some ants. She watched them listlessly. Wingless females, they were, with yellow abdomens so transparent in the sun she could see through them. They ran, following their own invisible paths, as though always trying to get somewhere quickly. She wondered what their hurry was. A child at home sick? A lover? She put sticks across their paths. At first they were disconcerted. One or two even climbed each other and the grass blades, as though to get a better view. Others backtracked and found a new way through the crevices and fissures of their mud landscape. Soon the stream was off again, the stick path, the obstacle, abandoned. She sat for a long time watching them.

Josie had unbuttoned her blouse because of the heat, and part of her breast showed. She no longer cared. She touched a bruise where Harry had bitten her. She knew she was burning, the skin felt tingly, even on her back, through her shirt. At last she got up, wiping the dust from her jodhpurs and looked around. She had been sitting beside the carcass of a sheep. Fly-blown and rotten, swollen and fetid, she had not heard the sound of the flies feasting on it. The ants were running in and out of its eyes. Now she was aware of it, the stench of the rotting meat overpowered her. She was violently sick.

When the retching finally stopped, Josie wiped her mouth on the tail of her blouse. She walked the horse to the next gate and when she felt stronger managed to hoist herself back onto it. She could see the silver of the poplars shimmering against the dark green pines at the Picnic Ground. Alien trees in this landscape, they had a depth and colour the native trees did not have. Yet they survived.

She would have a swim. Wash the dust and the smell of

sick and the smell of Harry from her. The horse's hooves were already in the shallow reaches of the river. Soft splashy noises of the Murrumbidgee. A flock of wild ducks took off noisily from the surface as they splashed on. Plovers flew. She came to the swimming hole and Josie let herself fall from the horse into the water turning over and over like a fish on a line. It felt so good, this ageless river, this life giving water. Her clothes, her skin, her hair, soaked it up. It offered her its own secrets, its own channel to the great sea. It would outlast all of them, this river, and when it sputtered and sank completely from view, and they thought it was gone for ever, that was when it was at its strongest. For it was still flowing, secretly coursing away under the ground, fed by springs hidden from their human eyes. And Josie's pores soaked up this secret and she cried into the river as she used to into Liz's back, but the river didn't turn away, just went on, warmly flowing, tumbling over her, keening with her, until the pain eased and she could resurface and think how to go on.

· EIGHTEEN ·

The execution of BB's original plan had been thwarted. She sat having her breakfast on Christmas Eve, gnashing her teeth and thinking. She had exhausted herself yesterday walking around with that big heavy oar and had pulled a muscle in her shoulder. She rubbed the spot now with one hand. It had been stupid of her to carry such a heavy thing. She could just as easily have left it behind. Anyway, she had mentioned it to Harry, that she would love to use the boat one day, and Reilley had taken the boat on the trailer down to the river's edge and she could use it later, if she wanted.

Alex's parentage festered in her mind. She could not stop returning to it and it had paled Daphne's visit into insignificance. Daphne. Everything about Daphne was paling for BB.

BB bit at her toast savagely. The silly old goat had signed all her savings over to Mr Doughty. She'd only found out about it last night. Half, they said was for a funeral fund for Daphne and the other half was supposedly for BB, but with Mr Doughty's name on it, what legal right would BB have? When the holiday was over she was going to go into the Building Society and have a look at those deposits. She knew the woman behind the counter quite well; she'd taken her a dish of risotto in the spring when they were both competing in the Lawn Bowling Championships. The only problem had been that the woman had been taken sick with the gastric on the eve of the match, and it was BB who had gone on to the finals. But she was sure she wouldn't hold that against her.

It made her feel sick herself to think that Mr Doughty had his hands on that money. Sticky as dough his fingers were, and just as hard to clean off. Dotty old woman, trusting him like that. Just because he's fed her some garbage about us getting married and him coming into the family. But he does hang on like a limpet so. Why do men always think they own you, when all you've done is accept a meal from them or a bit of friendship? It was beyond BB. When she sorted out her other problems, she would just have to sort him out too.

'May I have some toast, please?' asked Daphne.

Her teeth were out and she had to say it twice before BB could understand her. They were having a late breakfast in the kitchen. BB eyed the old lady as she sliced some bread.

'You look a mess,' she said. Daphne was still in her old terry towelling bath robe striped like a circus tent, nearly as big, and smelling of cat. BB realized with a twinge of regret that she had rather enjoyed having her breakfast on her own. Time then to sort out the plans for the day and talk to her budgie.

She popped the bread in the toaster and halved some passion fruit and pawpaw. The first few days after Daphne's arrival it had been rather fun to set up a tray with a pretty cloth (which was now in the wash – she'd never been through so many tray cloths in so few days!) She'd even run out and picked a ranuncula bloom the first morning and tucked it into the napkin. The tray had looked lovely, and sitting on the edge of her mother's bed, with the tea steaming between them and breathing in the early morning air with the scent of eucalyptus and listening to the bird sounds, why it had all been cosy and perfect. Just as she had imagined it. Daphne had asked the next morning if she could have a different brand of tea. She found this brand too strong. Too much tannin, she complained. She liked Earl Grey, which BB had to borrow from Liz's cupboard until she had time to go to

175

town. So now BB made two pots in the morning because she couldn't stand the smell of Earl Grey, let alone the taste of it. The trouble was the house wasn't her own any more. She had sneaked out of bed early one morning, imagine, tiptoeing through her own house, and gone to the kitchen for a cuppa and a snack, and at the first whistle of the kettle, before BB could lift it off the stove, Daphne had called out, 'Is that you dear? Are you making a cup of tea? Oh I would love one.' And BB had banged down the other metal teapot and shovelled in the tea leaves. There was no cloth on the tray that morning.

Daphne slept too lightly. If BB as much as turned over in her sleep, she would call out nervously. And the 'possums, who put on a fantastic club act each night, with their thumping, pounding, scratching and breathing, sent Daphne into near paroxysms of terror as they scampered overhead. BB told her crossly to put her head under the blankets the same as she did.

But the real difficulty was the bath. Daphne, with her size, her age and her bad hip working against her, found getting in and out of the bath very difficult. She had got quite stuck in the bathtub the first time she had used it. Since she had locked the door from the inside, BB had to climb through the small, high-up bathroom window, no mean feat, and even then it had taken some hauling to get Daphne out of the tub. BB realized she would probably have to put a shower in for her mother, and replace the louvered windows which she had broken climbing through. What a nuisance.

BB had no idea that her own routine would be so disrupted by Daphne's stay. 'I think,' she had said this morning at the door to Daphne's room, 'that you'll have to get up for breakfast. I can't keep running in and out with different things you want.' (They had been through the whole whistling kettle routine at six o'clock.)

'I only asked if you had some marmalade.'

'No, I don't have any marmalade. I have raspberry jam or nothing.'

'I can't eat raspberry. The seeds get under my plate.'

'Then eat with your teeth out,' said BB swirling her own dressing gown around her and going back to her own room. She had actually fallen back asleep and that was why they were late this morning.

BB buttered some toast, licking her fingers as she did. Her budgie chirped cheerfully. 'Here my little poppet,' said BB, cutting off a square and pushing it through the bars of the cage. 'Do you want a bit, Daphne?' Daphne took it gingerly from her fingers.

'Birds are for the birds,' she said. She munched carefully then threw down her toast. 'I can't eat without my teeth. Help me up.' They struggled with her cane and she went out and came in again and BB said, 'Now your toast is cold.'

'I miss my cat,' said Daphne as she picked up the halved passion fruit and poked at it suspiciously with her teaspoon. 'What's this then?'

'Eat it, it's good for you.'

'Funny looking fruit,' said Daphne.

BB leaned forward and said to Daphne, 'Promise you won't tell if I tell you something?'

'What?'

'Promise. Spit to die and cross your heart.'

'Oh for heaven's sake.' For a fleeting moment Daphne reminded BB of Liz.

BB hugged herself and waited.

'Oh all right then.' Daphne spat on the floor and crossed her heart.

BB rolled her words around her tongue like a last piece of toast. 'Josie told me the most amazing thing. She . . . told . . . me . . . that . . . Alex is not her husband's son!'

She sat back triumphantly.

Daphne had got a passion fruit seed stuck under the plate of her false teeth. She poked at it with her tongue and tried to draw it out with sheer suction.

'What? Who's son is he then?'

'Oh I'm not going to give up that little titbit.' BB wiped her own mouth with a napkin.

She wanted to use that piece of information in the future. It gave her such wonderful shivers up and down her spine when she thought how she would tell Liz. Would tell her right at the crucial moment, when Liz was being all snooty and cold to her. The next sharp thing Liz said to her, she'd whip it out. She'd never been able really to get at Liz before; Liz had always had her own secret strength. Now she knew, she could winkle it out, just as easily as getting a snail out of its shell with a hairpin.

'Why did she tell you that? When?' Daphne's mind which had been absorbed with the irritating seed, began to take in what BB was saying. Her mind began to clear. She stared at BB across the table. Daphne who was querulous, and sometimes senile, and often forgetful, was not a fool.

'Well she probably didn't mean to. It slipped out because we had a terrible row. It was at the picnic when you were asleep after lunch. And she told me, listen to this, that Alex is not a Jew. Her exact words were "You think you have a Jew for a grandson. I wish you did!"' Daphne said nothing but looked at her shrewdly. BB was beside herself with pleasure. 'Come to think of it, Alex looks nothing like Michael at all. I never did think much of Michael. He was dark, very dark with olive skin and eyes. Like my baby brother, Marco.'

'Bigot!' said Daphne spitting out the passion fruit seed at last.

'I am not!'

'You are and you're disgusting!' Daphne banged her stick on the floor. The budgie flew up in fright.

But BB was like a dog running with a rabbit in its mouth. There was no stopping her. 'I knew immediately she told me, what I had to do.'

'What do you have to do?'

'Alex is not a Jew. Never thought he was of course. He's one of us. Except for one thing.' She paused dramatically. 'He's not baptized.'

'Baptized! Baptized!' spluttered Daphne having difficulty with her words even with her teeth in.

'That's right, and I intend to fix that. Look.' She went to her overall hanging on the back of the kitchen door and took out a flat thick glass bottle with a cork in it. It was full of water.

'Holy water,' she said, holding it up, 'I got it from the church on Sunday when no-one was looking and I'm going to baptize my grandson with it and save his soul.'

Daphne stood up slowly, leaning heavily on her stick. She was quivering all over. 'BB. You cannot do this. You must not. I forbid you.'

'Forbid me? You?'

'None of it is any of your business. Give up this ridiculous idea.'

BB laughed, 'As you gave up me?'

'Oh, you have a cruel tongue BB. But, yes. As I gave up you.'

BB placed the bottle proudly on the table. 'You can't stop me.'

'I won't let you destroy that boy. If he doesn't know, it's not for you to tell him.'

'Oh shut up you old bag,' said BB, leaning back in her chair. 'Do you think I brought you all the way down here for you to tell me what to do? Don't start moralizing at me. Or I'll put you in a home. That's what I'll do. Don't think I won't.'

Daphne let out a long whoosh of rage through her false teeth. She swung up her stick suddenly so that BB ducked, and with amazing agility and strength, she swept the bottle of holy water to the floor. It smashed into sharp green fragments with a satisfying crash. The bird flew up in agitated squackings at the noise.

'Oh!' said BB. 'Oh!'

Daphne turned and walked out of the room and went into her own room and shut the door firmly. BB was on her knees muttering to herself, cleaning up the mess. Daphne was being very quiet she thought, listening with her head to one side. BB looked very like her bird when she did this. She heard a muffled bump or two and then Daphne opened her door again and BB threw herself back into the action of cleaning up. Daphne appeared in the doorway in her print dress with her hair neatly combed and her outdoor shoes on.

'I will not stay in this house with you,' she said. Her voice quivered but her head was up. 'I've packed my bags and I'll send someone up for them later. Please do not touch any of my things.'

'I wouldn't dream of it.' BB stuck her own chin in the air.

The old lady walked with her stick to the front door. BB jumped up from her knees and said, following her, not really believing she was going, 'I suppose you still want us to pick you up and take you to Mass tonight?'

Daphne had manoeuvred herself slowly down the two steps of the verandah past the clay pots of geraniums. She turned at the bottom and said, 'It would be a sacrilege to sit beside you in a church. I don't wish to come.'

'Please yourself then,' said BB leaning against the verandah post and folding her arms.

Daphne took her stick and before BB could stop her she had knocked the geraniums off the steps.

'Oh! Oh! You dreadful old woman!' BB rushed to her pots. Daphne gave the geraniums a few more whacks for good measure and stood on a particularly soft green one with a bronze tinge to its edges. 'My Sophia Dumaresque! Oh how could you do this? I've grown it from a cutting! Oh My Black Cox! And my Mabel Grey!' BB tried to take in this terrible disaster, picking up broken stems and leaves, and shards of clay pottery. But Daphne ignored her and her protestations, kicked a root ball out of her way, and catching her breath walked painfully and slowly and with much pride away from BB's house.

· NINETEEN ·

Midnight Mass.

Josie had not been to one in years. She supposed she ought to dress properly for it, a neat dress, stockings, gloves. As she pulled on her stockings and snapped them to her suspender belt she thought it was the first time since she arrived that she had done so. There was a looseness that the heat brought to people who lived in it. She resented now the constricting and heating of her flesh under the clothes. She did not want to go to Mass with BB. But there was no way out of it that she could see. And Liz had put out on her bed, an old childhood missal and a choice of headscarves, so it all seemed to be settled.

She had arrived back at the Big House, her own thoughts in turmoil, her body still remembering Harry's lovemaking, to find Daphne weeping into her handkerchief in the hallway. She had collapsed on the bottom stair, her hot, red flushed face contrasting with the blue of the carpet, and Liz trying to comfort her. Josie was glad of the distraction. Daphne wouldn't talk except to say through sobs that BB was a cruel woman and she would much rather live with Mr Doughty, whom she trusted, and who did after all remind her of her own dear departed Porry, God Rest His Soul, who had never, never let a cruel word pass his lips in all the years they had been married. But she didn't want to go into it and she would never speak to BB ever again. Never. And Liz said they would discuss it all tomorrow when everybody was more calm and why didn't Daphne just get up and she would help her into the small room upstairs that had been Harry's mother's where she could spend the night? And indeed Daphne had soon fallen asleep after a hot glass of milk liberally laced with whisky and with the comforting weight of Liz's cat purring on her feet.

'I knew it would come to this! I knew it!' Liz kept repeating as she dialled her mother's number for an explanation. But BB just hung up when she mentioned Daphne's name. Dinner was a melancholy affair, even the food seemed cheerless, the wine dispirited. Josie and Harry avoided each other's eyes and Liz was beside herself with anger over BB's treatment of Daphne. She suspected their argument had something to do with money and Mr Doughty, and that BB had taken any excuse as a way of dumping Daphne now the newness of the experiment was over. Harry got up abruptly halfway through his dessert, one of his favourites, summer pudding, and said he was going out to shoot rabbits. Which surprised Liz but she said nothing. Alex went with him, and the sisters sat and listened to the truck roar and saw the headlights beam across the lower paddocks.

They felt bereft, thrown on each other's company, with so many land mines to be avoided in their conversation. So they sat quietly and finished their wine and clicked their spoons against the cool moons of plates and licked the sweetness off their lips. And all the time they swallowed words and phrases that rose like bitter bile into their mouths. Once Liz said, 'I'd like to have new curtains in this room,' and they discussed possibilities. And Josie said something about last Christmas which she had spent in Florida with Michael's parents. And talking of old people got them back to Daphne, so they had come full circle in their conversation. And when they had exhausted that topic they got up from the table and cleared it and while they were in the kitchen they talked about Cynthia and Liz hoped she'd feel better tomorrow because she didn't know how she would cope otherwise, and then they saw the headlights of the truck coming back and they both expelled deep sighs which showed they had been holding their breath all along. Their men had bagged two rabbits, and Harry showed Alex how to gut and skin them at the sink while they were still warm. Alex grasped the pelt firmly and it slipped off like a glove. Liz took the small bluish bodies in her hands and wrapped them in paper and put them in the 'fridge. She would cook them on Boxing Day she said. It would make a pleasant change from mutton or leftover turkey. And Josie said it was probably time she went up and changed for church and Liz took the car keys from the top of the 'fridge and dropped them into her palm as though they were hot.

When she arrived at BB's house, after driving carefully up the unfamiliar road, Josie found BB already dressed and waiting for her on her verandah. She had on a black, sleeveless dress, quite elegant in contrast to her usual clothes, but an odd colour choice for a feast day, Josie thought. Neither of them wished to be alone with the other in the car, and it seemed as though the earlier silence of dinner had carried over into the station wagon. For this small mercy, Josie was grateful, and after the first stilted question and answer (BB wanting to know if Daphne had said anything, and Josie saying, no, but she had telephoned Mr Doughty), they both sat busy with their own thoughts, and not until they reached the edge of the town and crossed the main highway, did BB sit up and take notice and start to direct Josie to the church.

At the church, a new blonde brick and wooden structure in hexagonal shape, the congregation was buzzing with good cheer and Christmas excitement and nearly all the pews were taken. Mr Doughty, who was a gentleman, even if he was a bore, was waiting for them in the vestibule. BB's eyes swept through him as if he were not there.

'I've kept a couple of seats at the front,' he said to Josie. 'It always fills up early on Christmas Eve.'

BB also spoke to Josie. 'I have an errand to do,' she said, 'in the sanctuary. I won't be a minute.'

Mr Doughty and Josie were abandoned in the stream of people coming into the church. The people flowed around them in the small vestibule in a moist surge of perspiration, body odour and perfume. The strains of organ music rose and fell from the brightly lit church. Mr Doughty said that Daphne had telephoned him and he felt very badly about all this trouble. He just hoped he wasn't the cause of it. He was, after all only trying to help Daphne protect her money, he knew a little bit about these things, and hadn't realized BB would take it as a personal affront to her own interests. Josie nodded sympathetically. People were jamming in around them. Tired children, already yawning before the service began, complained to their parents about the lack of seats; the little girls with their hair stretched back in rubber bands and ribbons, which made bumps under their hats and gave them headaches; the boys, with slicked down hair, grimacing as they stretched their necks inside unfamiliar collars. Mr Doughty was just telling Josie that he had bought a book of Banjo Paterson's poetry for Alex for Christmas when BB came bustling back through the throng.

'Just in time,' said Mr Doughty to Josie. Josie wondered if she were going to be the transmitter all night. BB hugged her commodious handbag to her chest and said to Josie, 'We can go in now.'

Mr Doughty led the way down the centre aisle, his soft grey suit rumpled in the back. BB followed him, a discordant dark figure in a sea of summer clothes, a small black straw hat like a three-fingered starfish clutching her head. Josie tied a scarf under her chin, and they squeezed into a row that Mr Doughty indicated, the space obligingly kept by a round, fat nun who smiled at Josie from beneath her wimple and moved over an inch as she sat down. But BB objected to having to sit next to Mr Doughty and so they all shuffled around until

Josie was again the meat in the sandwich between them.

A choir of towheaded boys and girls sang self-consciously in front of a small electric organ. The altar was lit with many candles, and the heat of the flames added to the heat of the massed bodies in the church. Steam was rising from the black serge habit of BB's neighbour. The bodies pressed together made the air inside the church humid, and the dampness picked up the scents of the flowers spilling over their copper vases beside the altar. The heavy heads of full-blown garden roses, no mean hybrids here, intermingled with the blue branches of young round eucalyptus leaves, and stiff stalks of yellow gladioli vied with delphiniums to reach the ceiling. BB whispered that the Ladies Auxiliary had done themselves proud this year. Under the headiness of the flowers' perfume, Josie could detect the plain soap smell of the nun, BB's muskiness, Mr Doughty's mild cologne, and the faintest hint of Harry coming from her own body.

The flames of the candles flickered upwards and joined the lights in the wooden vaulting of the ceiling. The light poured down on them. It was all too bright thought Josie. All too light; the white interior of the church, the bleached wooden pews, the pale upper arms of the women where their short sleeves showed the demarcation from washing line tans to pale intimacy. It was a white blandness that struck Josie anew and reminded her of the youth of the country she was in. Not Cynthia's country, but theirs, their white Australia. There had been no time for smoke to rub into these walls; for the oil of bodies and the sweat of clothes to darken these seats; for an influx of different people to mix the blood of the worshippers. It was all too homogenous. And it was a place she had once been familiar with. But no longer. She felt a stranger here. All the surfaces were exposed in the blinding glare, the grain of the wood, the pores of a cheek, the woven mesh of a panama hat. Josie felt she was again out on the river flats with the sun beating down on her, her breasts exposed, and all the congregation knowing of her adultery. They were mocking her behind the trees, from the banks of the river, even lying low in the stubbly grass of Harry's failed lucerne crop. The only escape from the merciless light was behind one's fingers in an atittude of prayer.

The congregation rose when the priest, probably Father Murphy, entered in his white Yuletide vestments. The brocade chasuble shimmered like a mirage as he moved to his position and waited for the two altar boys to join him. Josie opened the missal that Liz had lent her. It was one she had had at school and inside in large handwriting Liz had written Elizabeth Beauchamp, May 31st, 1942. Liz's twelfth birthday. A Sunday. Memory, like a bubble, rose to the surface of Josie's mind. There was something that BB had said the other day. Josie struggled with her mind while one part listened to the opening liturgy of the Mass. The bubble burst to the surface. Yes. A beautiful day, a moonlit night when BB was intent on a young man with a wisp of growth on his upper lip. The rings spread. Memory rushed, ever widening and encompassing, over Josie standing in the brilliance with the missal in her hand.

'Do you think she is going to surprise us?' Josie had asked, skipping up the street and into their garden path behind her sister.

'I don't know, what do you think?' Liz was striding along, stepping over the broken concrete path, the straggling weeds, the squashed bits of paper blown in from the street.

'She might be going to,' she went on. 'It is my birthday and she didn't say anything about it this morning. Not anything.' They had spent the day with a schoolfriend on the North Shore, had got up early that morning while BB was still in bed. She had got in late the night before. She had mumbled to them and thrown the covers over her head when they told her they were off and they had put their bathers and towels into their school satchels, although really they thought it would be too cold to swim.

Josie remembered the feeling of running with happiness as they came home. They had spent the day with Marjorie or Margaret or Mary, she couldn't quite remember the girl's name now. The girl was one of seven children, six of them boys, with a timid, tired mother and an authoritarian father, who, thankfully, had not been there that day. They had spent days there before and it was always bad luck to be caught by him in the afternoon, particularly if one was going to the pictures, or just out for an ice with some friends, because he always picked that as a good time for the family to gather for the Rosary and they would all have to kneel down and pray. And it was an agony of impatience waiting for him to get through with it. Marjorie, yes, it was Marjorie, had given Liz the missal, her Dad's idea, she had apologized, and then produced a small bunch of violets tied with a ribbon of her own and said, Happy Birthday.

'There's probably a chocolate cake and candles. And she's probably finished that dress for you. Oh, it's going to look lovely on you with your boosies and everything.' And with a sigh, 'I wish I was twelve.'

They pushed open the bottom door and the usual whiff of leaking gas and stale cooking smells met them. But that was a home smell they were used to. They ran for the stairs trying to beat each other up to their landing. The door of their apartment was locked. Josie knocked and chattered on. 'I wish I was old enough to wear that dress. She nearly finished it last night before she went out. I saw it on the sewing machine this morning. What time does the play start? Oh, Liz won't it be nice if Mum comes too? And on your birthday?' They knocked on the door loudly. There was no reply.

Liz swung her brown leather satchel off her back and rummaged for the key. 'Here, hold this.' She handed Josie the bunch of violets. 'I've only got one line to say, Josie. Just to

announce the play you know. I'm not playing Lady Macbeth.'
But Josie was excited. 'Everyone will be looking at you, and
you'll be all alone in front of the curtain. Oh! What shoes
will you wear?' Liz had put the key in the lock and just as
she was turning it the apartment door opposite theirs opened
and the tenant, a foul-mouthed and bad-tempered alcoholic,
stuck his head out and glared at them. 'Can't you keep the
bleedin' noise down and let a bugger get some sleep?' 'Sorry,'
the girls said putting their upper teeth on their lower lips.
'And yer Mum's out, so shut up or I'll come in and belt yer.'
He withdrew his head and slammed the door. The girls looked
at each other and tiptoed in closing their own door softly.
'Crabby,' said Liz sticking out her tongue when she felt she
was safe.

Josie ran into the kitchen. She put the violets on the table.
She opened the refrigerator door. 'It must be somewhere,' she
said. She ran to the pantry, opened the cupboard doors,
looked into the bread bin. 'There isn't one.' Her voice was
puzzled. 'There isn't a cake, Liz,' she turned to her sister
helplessly. Liz was standing in the doorway of the kitchen,
her satchel hanging down beside her legs. There was a hole
in her sock. 'She's probably gone out to buy one,' Josie said.
'We're back early, that's all.' She ran past her sister into
the sitting room where the treadle sewing machine stood
dominating one wall. Lying on it, crumpled, untouched since
the night before, was the dress Liz was to wear. Josie rushed
to it and grabbed it, holding it up, looking at the bodice, still
held to the skirt by pins. She threw it down on the machine.
'Oh, Liz. Your part!' Liz was still standing in the hallway.
She looked at her younger sister.

'She forgot.' Her voice was old.

'Oh I thought at least there would be a cake, Liz?'

Liz threw her satchel along the hall at Josie.

'Oh, shut up about the cake, will you? Just shut up about
it.'

She stormed into the bedroom they shared and threw herself on the bed. Josie could hear her pounding on the bed with her fists. She stood frightened beside the bed and whispered, 'What about the play?'

'I'm not going.'

After what seemed a long time, Liz got up and came into the kitchen and opened a can of salmon. Josie put the violets, now bedraggled, in a glass of water on the oilcloth. Josie poked at the salmon on her plate with her fork. 'They say there are bits of glass in the salmon. The Japs put them there they say.'

'It's not true. Just eat up.'

Josie pushed her plate away. 'I'm not very hungry,' she said.

'Neither am I.'

They spent a miserable night. Once they heard the floor creaking outside and they held their breath until they heard their neighbour stumbling his way down the stairs. They had gone to bed, turning away from each other; Liz not wanting to be comforted; Josie not knowing how to offer it when she kept being rebuffed. They were listening to the water sounds of the Harbour, the creaks of the old apartment building. The moon was flooding the room with light when suddenly there was an enormous explosion which shook the building and made their windows rattle. Josie screamed and Liz rushed to the window. Loud deep booms followed the first explosion. 'Look. Look.' The sky was lit with searchlights and a huge red flare went up like a firework. 'It's the Japs,' said Josie trembling beside Liz at the window. They could see nothing outside now but darkness. They could hear other voices, in the street, in the houses around them. 'It must be the Japs,' said Liz, 'invading.' Josie began to cry. 'Oh Mummy, where are you?'

'Don't be such a baby,' said Liz.

They got back into bed and held each other listening to

the sounds of the people in the street, waiting for more explosions. But there were none. Gradually the murmuring noise of the people subsided. The girls must have fallen asleep for Liz woke Josie with a shake. There were faint noises from the sitting room, muffled, indistinct. Liz got out of bed. Josie was behind her, holding on to her nightgown. Liz opened the door and they tiptoed to the open door of the sitting room. They could see along the hall, a lit tableau, a corner of the kitchen table on which stood two half-finished glasses of beer, a broken bunch of violets.

A faint light shone out of the sitting room. At first they could see nothing and then in the gloom, they could make out the big chair near the radiator and they could see their mother. She was sitting on someone's knee. They couldn't see his face, for she was kissing him. But it was a soldier, they could see his laced up shoe and the colour of his trousers. Their mother's skirt was up, they could see the soldier's hand on her thigh, the fleshy gap above her rolled stocking top. The couple were oblivious to them. Their mother put her head back, her new blonde head, and there were dark violets in it that her lover had placed there. Josie saw one fall to the floor, soft, soft, like it weighed nothing and was falling through thick water.

Liz turned away and they went silently back to bed. They said nothing to each other. Josie remembered her mother on her father's knee. Josie clung to Liz. 'She did forget, didn't she?' she whispered.

'Go to sleep.' Josie listened to Liz's breathing beside her for a while and then she did fall asleep, until, turning over in the night, her cheek touched her sister's damp pillow and it woke her up.

Dampness on her cheek.

Josie realized they were her own tears now, as she knelt, listening to the Latin words murmuring from the altar. So

191

powerful was the hold of her memories, that she touched the wedding ring on her left hand to reassure herself in what time she was. She was conscious of BB's greying-brown head now bowed beside her.

'Filius meus es tu, ego hodie genui te.'

'Thou art my son, this day I have begotten Thee.'

In the privacy of her templed fingers, Josie thought about her own son. She had tried so hard to be a good mother to him, to be more than BB had been to her and Liz. When he was a baby, even the white milk spittle on her shoulder had been a love sign. And once, in a restaurant where the sun came through the window, she had held him up above her head and a long thread of golden saliva had fallen from his lips and touched her own and had made her womb contract with such anguish that she had handed him to Michael. As he had grown, she had been determined not to repeat BB's examples of motherhood. On rainy wet days she would hurry to the bus stop to meet him after school with his yellow coat, an umbrella, a pair of overshoes. Her feet were soaking but she did not mind. The small hand slipping into her own, the surprised delight at her unexpected appearance, were like putting on socks, warmed beside a fire.

BB, sitting like a black shadow beside her, stirred as though she knew what Josie was thinking. The pain that BB had inflicted on them over the years, not the pain of physical beating but the destruction of innocent trust, had left its mark. How close she had come to following the same pattern. How different Liz might have been.

My son, my son.

'In the brightness of the saints, from the womb before the day star I begot Thee.'

Oh sweet Jesus, Sanctus. I have been no better than BB. How could I have been so blind. A tear fell down Josie's cheek, escaped from under her fingers. It plopped on the pale wood of the pew. The choir swelled and she looked up. The luminosity of the candles seemed to grow until the light poured over her like a truth revealed. Her eyes were washed by the light. There is no way for me to put things right, thought Josie. I can't undo the past. That's what Harry meant. It isn't there we make changes. It is in the future. Josie's finger touched the wet stain on the pew.

The bells rang for the most secret Mystery of the Mass. They had always made Josie shiver, and they made her shiver now. For she knew what she had to do.

And Josie Rosenbloom, who believed, bowed her head at the bells, and accepted, that just as that one night in Sydney had changed her mortal life forever, she accepted that it had claimed her immortal soul too.

Mr Doughty got up and joined the line for communion. The nun stepped across Josie and BB with a smiled apology and a whiff of Sunlight soap. BB with her divorces, and in spite of all her confessions, could not go up to the altar. Josie sat quietly with her hands in her lap. The light had gone dull and flat.

The people came back. They knelt briefly. When they sat, BB's and Mr Doughty's thighs burned through the material of their clothes into Josie's own. She thought of her passion that afternoon with Harry. She would never stop loving him. She knew that now. But she could not have him. The harsh light offered no comfort. The choir sang.

The offertory plate came around. She opened her bag for money and felt with her fingers the edge of the envelope, the letter she had written to Michael. How she had carried it with her like a bad conscience. Her money fell softly on the green baize bottom of the wooden bowl. It was a bit like her heart, bruised tissue onto which the points of barbs or lances were now blunted.

She suddenly wanted to see Alex, wanted to touch him. She waited now with impatience for the Mass to finish, the last hymn to be sung. She glanced at BB and BB, feeling her gaze, looked back, her eyes full of limpid self-satisfaction. It was a look that ricocheted off Josie for she knew now who her enemy was. And it was BB. BB to whom she should never have divulged her secret. Because BB could not be trusted. BB would follow her own twisted path to righteousness.

After Josie said goodnight to Mr Doughty, who was coming to Christmas dinner tomorrow anyway, BB and Josie drove back to Tiddalik. Thin clouds obscured the stars and the moon and BB sniffed the air like a spaniel. 'I think we're going to have rain tomorrow.'

'About Alex,' said Josie firmly, gripping the steering wheel.

BB went silent.

'You are never, never to repeat what I told you. Do you understand?'

Beside her in the dark, BB held her handbag to her chest like a shield.

'I mean it BB, if you as much as breathe a word, to him, or to anyone else; I'll kill you.' She could feel BB tensing on the seat beside her and she knew quite dispassionately, for the first time in her life, that she could be capable of great violence; that she could tear BB limb from limb with her hands, if she hurt her son.

Josie felt she had been squeezed through the waist of an egg timer these last few days. She suddenly pulled the car over and stopped and BB shrank further back into the seat as though Josie was about to carry out her threat immediately. Josie took the letter from her handbag and tore it into pieces. She did not explain her actions to her mother. She did not have to any more. She put the car back into gear and, as they rolled down the hill, she let the pieces flutter from her fingers out the window, and she could see them in her rear vision mirror like small white birds whipped up, scattered by their passage along the country road. How clear and simple everything was as she drove down the winding road into the valley of the Murrumbidgee. The car lights picked up the white painted posts that guarded them from the drop below. One, one, one, the posts went by, marking the distance, just as her mind, marking distance and time had fallen like grains of sand from one understanding to another. She had thought in the hourglass portion of her life before, that sharing her secret would dissolve the tensions under which she lived. How stupid, she thought, when the opposite was true. There was only herself after all to rely on, only herself to blame if she failed.

The headlights of the car picked up the steel beams of the Tarago Bridge over the Murrumbidgee. For a moment the moon came out behind the cloud cover and the trickle of the once mighty river below them could be seen. BB said as they crossed it, 'Oh how dry it has been. What a change is coming.' She moved her hands over her bag and the sound reminded Josie of dead leaves rustling together. They said no more to each other except Goodnight when Josie dropped her off at Top House. She parked the car in the garage of the Big House and picked her way lightly across the garden. Inside, her hand traced the walls, the edge of a painting, the carving of the newel post. She tiptoed up the stairs, grimacing at the creaks of the old treads. Under the one lamp left burning in the upper hall, hundreds of small insects lay dead on the floor and the table. Josie went into Alex's room, leaving the door to the hall ajar. She could just make out his form in the dark. She felt his toes under the single sheet.

'Mom?' His voice was sleepy.

'Yes, it's me,' she whispered. 'Just come to say goodnight.'

He rolled over, his torso bare because of the heat, his arm, not boy, not man, thrown over his pillow. She bent to kiss his ear. The lobe was softer than the leaf of an African violet. It tingled her lips. Ah, yes, she thought, it would be enough.

'Goodnight, son,' she said. He mumbled, half-asleep, his eyes shut, his body turned away.

'Mom? Dad called.'

'Oh that's nice. What did he say?'

'*Shalom*, he said. Just tell Mom, *Shalom*.'

He fell back into sleep and she sat listening to his deep breathing. She pulled the sheet gently up over his bare shoulder. She stood up and the room swayed for a moment. She heard the bellowing outside of the cattle, and the undercurrent of the cicadas, and then the cicadas seemed to swell, until their small noise drowned out all others and she felt the noise was so deafening that everyone must awake. But they did not. Only she was listening. She went out of the room, switched off the lamp in the hall. She leaned her forehead for a moment against the wall, the wall of Harry's and Liz's room. She was in a strange house in a strange country where she did not belong. How much time had she wasted trying to find that out?

· TWENTY ·

Alexander Rosenbloom, twelve years old, would never forget the first Christmas dinner he spent with his mother's family in the Big House at Tiddalik.

There were eleven of them sitting around the massive table in the dining room. The panelled walls of jarrah wood, hung with black framed prints of old Chinese ships, seemed even darker in the late afternoon gloom. It had been overcast all day, the rain threatening but never falling. All day Uncle Harry had kept going to the door, looking at the sky and testing the wind with his finger. By five o'clock, when they sat down to dinner after nibbling at salted peanuts and drinking mimosas in the drawing room, which the adults had drunk out of small green Bristol glasses, and Alex and the twins had been allowed a half glass each, the dampness hung in the air like a thick curtain.

Alex had helped Liz decorate this room this afternoon, trailing ivy and tinsel around the mantelpiece and hanging balloons from the centre of the bay windows at the far end of the room. Now the balloons hung listlessly against the Victorian stained glass. Not the slightest breeze came in though the olive coloured velvet curtains were pulled back wide, and only the fly meshing kept the dusk at bay. They had thrown a white damask tablecloth across the table, and lacking an abundance of flowers, Liz had laid ivy along the centre of the table too, where it glistened and gleamed in competition with the silver candlesticks and the footed dishes of sugared almonds, like dark green water on a moonlit beach.

Alex was sitting facing the fireplace between his mother and his Great Granny Daphne. One of the carved legs of the ornate table was in his way. He could feel it with his knees no matter which way he moved his legs. In moments of boredom, which adults seemed to induce easily in him these days, Alex would push his fingers in and out of a burn hole in the seat of his chair, feeling the prickly horsehair stuffing under the leather, so different from the foam padding he knew from home. He pulled out a long steel grey hair, which seemed to have no end, and he dropped it, hoping no one would notice, under the table.

'Now, young Alex,' said his Uncle Harry suddenly from the head of the table, 'pull this Christmas cracker with me.' Alex got up and went around his mother to pull the bon-bon with his uncle. Alex won his, and there was a whistle on a string inside and a riddle in French which no-one could work out. Then they all pulled their Christmas crackers, putting on ridiculous crêpe paper hats with silver and gold foil cutouts on them. They all looked pretty funny, though Alex still thought his Uncle Harry looked handsome in his.

The girl cousins, One and Two, were giggling over their riddles, which Alex, having spent a little time with them, realized meant they did not understand them either. The girls flanked BB like two speckled book ends. Alex had brought over a record from the States for them, an Allen Sherman record, called *My Son the Folk Singer*. He hoped they appreciated it. They had given him a sheepskin rug for his room back home. He imagined putting his toes into it on a cold winter morning. He had also been given a pen and pencil set from BB, with the message, *The Moving Finger Writes*, scribbled on the card. He asked his mother what it meant, and she said, nobody ever knew what BB meant. And Mr Doughty had given him a book of poems by someone called Banjo Paterson, and had inscribed inside the words of a ballad he'd found in an old copy of the *Sydney Bulletin*, which began;

We have all of us read how the Israelites fled
From Egypt with Pharoah in eager pursuit of 'em
And Pharoah's fierce troops were all put in the soup
When the waters rolled softly o'er every galoot of 'em.

He hadn't had time to read the rest, but it was all good rollicking stuff. Even Cynthia had given him a present, which was really neat, the sloughed off skin of a snake, a wondrous brittle skein of spangled diamonds, that she had come across in her garden. His mother had thought it was a hideous present and wouldn't touch it, but Alex had coiled it carefully back in the stocking box it had come in. He would have said that was the best present, if he hadn't received a stock whip of kangaroo hide from Aunt Liz and Uncle Harry. It even made the watch which his parents had given him, and which he had wanted for a long time, seem very tame.

Aunt Liz lit the candles on the table and the mantelpiece. They flickered and threw early shadows in the long room. Aunt Liz looked very beautiful, he thought, looking at her with new interest as she leaned towards him to light the candles with a long taper. The shadows threw circles under her eyes, but he had never seen her before in a good dress, a dark red silk with the sleeves cut away and her hair pinned up, so that a pair of lustrous diamond and baroque pearl earrings, that Harry's mother had given to her on her wedding day, glimmered in the light.

Cynthia brought in a huge tureen of cold pumpkin soup and put it on the mahogany side table. Aunt Liz got up again from her place at the far end of the table in front of the bay windows to serve it, ladling it with a large silver spoon into pale green dishes.

Aunt Liz was in a strange mood today, thought Alex still

watching her covertly. She always spoke in a staccato fashion, which suited her, there was after all a spareness about her style that was oddly attractive. But today she had been even more abrupt than usual. He had met her coming out of the upstairs bathroom first thing this morning, with her eyes red and her face white, and she had said as she passed him on the way to her room, one word, 'Ruby'. But he knew that was not true. He had heard her snap at Cynthia in the kitchen over some trivial detail, and watched Cynthia, who knew how to handle these things, look at the ceiling for help and then squeeze her lips together so that her face looked comical. Except she made sure Aunt Liz didn't see. And then, when he was blowing up balloons in the dining room, and Aunt Liz was laying the table, he had caught her looking at him with an expression on her face he had not seen there before. He could not say exactly what the expression was but it reminded him of longing; he had sometimes seen it on his father's face too when his father looked at his mother, which was how he could identify it. It embarrassed him to see it on his aunt's face and when his aunt realized he had seen her with her mask down, she had suddenly dropped the silver on the table and rushed across the room and hugged him to her, for no reason, and then left the room holding the heels of her hands to her temples. He had heard a Whisht! at the window and turned around to see BB beckoning him through the fly screen and he had gone over to find out what she wanted when his aunt came back into the room, recovered from her indiscretion, and BB had dropped from sight like a child playing hiding games. He couldn't understand any of them, to be truthful.

Cynthia carefully placed a bowl of yellow soup in front of him. It looked thick and pasty. He thought about his aunt. His mother had told him his aunt was 'artistic', perhaps that was it, and yet, he thought as he watched Cynthia carry the bowls around the table, Aunt Liz had not reacted the way he thought she would when his mother gave her her Christmas present this morning. Alex had thought it was magnificent — a great box of oil colours, tubes and tubes inviting to be squeezed. Aunt Liz had merely nodded and put it at the bottom of her pile of presents. Uncle Harry had given Liz a red, silk kimono embroidered with chrysanthemums. He had had it sent from Hong Kong, he said. His aunt got up from the floor without a word, they were all sitting around the tree in an orgy of present opening with piles of paper and ribbon around them, and she had gone out of the room in her sensible blue dressing gown, and come back in a few minutes, blowing her nose. 'Cold,' she said.

The twins were wrinkling their noses up at the soup. 'Don't waste it on them,' said Aunt Julie who was sitting on Uncle Harry's left. Alex wished his mother would say the same thing, as he tasted the cold, glutinous mixture, but she was talking across Uncle Harry to Aunt Julie, gesturing with her slim bare arms, her silver bracelet winking in the candle-light as the room grew darker. On his right, Great Granny Daphne was sipping her soup slowly. She leaned very far forward to get it into her mouth without spilling. She had hardly said a word all afternoon, except to say, 'Thank you', when Alex hung her stick on the back of her chair when she sat down. Mr Doughty had held the chair out for her and BB had made a humphing sound which everyone ignored. But Daphne watched BB's lips closely, as though she were on guard to stop any words from falling out, of which she might disapprove.

The adults had opened another bottle of wine and Uncle Bob, sitting on the other side of the table on Aunt Liz's right, stood up to propose a toast.

'On behalf of us all, I want to thank Liz for a wonderful Christmas Dinner . . .'

'We haven't had it yet,' interrupted BB.

'. . . And I want to say welcome to our family from

overseas, Daphne and Josie and Alex. You ought to come more often . . .'

'Get on with it, Bob, or the turkey will be overcooked,' said Aunt Julie.

'Here here. Here here,' said Mr Doughty on his own.

'. . . And furthermore I want to propose a toast that this weather change is really going to come and break this bloody drought and make nineteen sixty-three a damn sight better, I mean, wetter than nineteen sixty-two. Cheers.'

'Cheers!'

'Bottoms up!'

'My God, this is a damn good drop, Harry.'

They all raised their glasses, which were misty in the humidity, and the children raised their own pink glasses of Ribena – another taste Alex could not get used to.

'I wonder what it will bring, nineteen sixty-three?' mused BB, looking right at Alex who found her gaze disconcerting. She was sitting almost directly opposite him with her small head under its crêpe paper crown framed by the black square of the fireplace. Her gold splashed spectacles hung from a chain around her neck like a bib on her thin chest.

Cynthia came in and began to clear the plates away.

Alex's mother said, after a sharp glance at BB; 'Well, you'll probably have English in the Mass. I was thinking last night that it might be the last Christmas Catholics celebrate in Latin.'

'Oh what rubbish,' said BB. 'I hope I don't live to see it.'

'But it's probably right,' said Aunt Liz. 'It's the number one topic on the agenda at the Vatican Council. And it won't make anyone a damn sight better.'

'We'll have television in our house next year,' said one of the twins, 'won't we Dad?'

'I'd like to have seen the Queen,' said Daphne, 'giving her Christmas speech.'

'You will be able to, next year,' said Uncle Bob. 'They've

started transmitting from Canberra this week. But I wonder if there will still be a Commonwealth? We might be a bloody republic by then. I mean, what do you think Harry, if Britain does go into the Common Market, where does that leave us? And I mean us bloody farmers? Hit us the worst, won't it, with those European subsidies? Where am I going to sell my bloody wool?'

He and Mr Doughty and Uncle Harry began talking seriously along the length of the table. Aunt Liz got up and went to get the 'magic maid' with Cynthia. Alex had never heard this phrase before and watched with interest for their return, but it was only an old heated food trolley which they wheeled in, and the disappointment must have shown on his face because he saw his cousins giggling at him. He pretended to be very interested in his napkin.

Uncle Harry got up to carve the huge golden turkey and the smoked ham covered with pineapple circles and cherries. Aunt Liz placed a plate of food in front of Alex. From the carving fork she dangled a piece of ham over his plate. The slice quivered and glistened in front of him.

'Do you want some?'

He looked at his mother.

She hesitated for a moment and said, 'No, just eat your turkey, Alex.'

BB made a tutting sound from the other side of the table. Daphne hissed.

The twin called One, looked at him drolly.

'Can't you eat ham?'

'I'm Jewish,' said Alex. 'Well, half anyway.'

'Which half?' asked the twin in her slow voice.

'That's enough,' said Uncle Bob. 'Eat your dinner.'

BB's head was quivering like a locust on a gum leaf. Alex noticed that all the adults were watching her, but he couldn't work out why, she looked just the same as always to him, her eyes now not settling on anything or anyone. She went on cutting up her food on her plate, playing with it, not eating it. He wondered if she were feeling the heat perhaps like the rest of them. Even Alex today was uncomfortable. When he raised his leg an inch from the leather seat, he could feel his pants sticking to it. But no, his grandmother looked cool, only her coal-coloured eyes looked hot reflecting in their pupils the flame of the candles. He glanced sideways at his mother and saw there was a thin film of perspiration above her lip.

When everyone was finally served and they had all settled down again, BB said;

'There's no such thing as an atheist.' She said it as though she had come to a great decision while cutting up her food. 'I've thought about it and thought about it, and there's no such thing. People merely find out as they grow older that their childhood beliefs are not enough. When it comes to the crunch, you'll all go back to Him, you wait. I've tried to give Him up over the years, it would have been much easier if I could have, but He won't let go. They went to Padua once, my parents, never took me, but they brought me back a relic of St Antony, a bone chip no bigger than the paring of a fingernail. Papa told me there was a relic of St Antony's tongue in the cathedral. That kept me quiet for days, I can tell you, I was afraid to open my mouth. But St Antony's chip, they put it in a locket for me and I wore it around my neck. I could pray to him for lost things. St Antony, St Antony, help me.'

Alex wanted to ask his grandmother what she had lost but he knew the answer would be complicated and a shared glance with his Uncle Harry told him they were both thinking the same thing. BB was oblivious to them, her mind like a fish darting around a sea anemone. 'One Sunday on the way to Mass,' she went on, 'I found a sack of kittens on the roadside. Someone had thrown them from a car and I wanted to keep them. But I couldn't go home with them and I couldn't take them to Mass. So I threw them in the village pond and ran on to Chapel. I looked over my shoulder and the bag just sat there on the surface like a bubble that wouldn't burst and I could hear them mewing. All through Communion I could hear them mewing. After Mass I ran to the pond but the bag was gone. I was so relieved that God hadn't punished me that I did a little dance in the street. And then St Antony jabbed me in the throat.' BB put down her knife and fork and touched her throat as though the locket were still there.

'Now, now, BB,' Mr Doughty said indulgently, hopelessly out of his depth but still trying to get back into BB's grace, 'It's Christmas, not a time for regret. Don't go all philosophical on us.'

'Oh, do shut up. I'm not talking about philosophy. I'm talking about religion and faith. You just mind your money and I'll mind my soul.'

'You don't have one,' said Daphne suddenly.

'And you won't have any money if you let him handle it.'

'Hold on a minute,' said Mr Doughty.

'That's a bit rough, isn't it?' said Uncle Bob.

'I'm only trying to help her invest it wisely,' said Mr Doughty.

'I wonder,' said BB.

Cynthia put her head around the door.

'There's a phone call from America for you, Mrs Rosenbloom.' Alex's mother put down her napkin and left the table.

Alex glanced at his new watch. He had put it on New York time because he liked the feeling of living in two time zones at once. It was a funny time for a call, he thought, since it was two in the morning in New York.

'The Church of Christ is a great thing to believe in,' went on BB as though there had been no interruption.

Great Granny Daphne's knife and fork clattered on her plate.

'BB,' she said, 'Stop it!' Amazingly, BB did. Aunt Liz took a long drink from her glass of wine.

'Proselytizing as always,' she said.

The faintest breeze came through the windows, not enough to stir the heavy velvet drapes but it picked up a tendril of Liz's hair which had come loose from her chignon. She tucked it up with her fingers under her party hat and the draped sleeve of her dark red silk dress swung open and Alex could see the under part of her arm, which seemed softer and more rounded than the rest of her body. Voluptuous he thought, and blushed as his mind said the word.

His mother came back in and they all swung their heads to look at her.

'It was Michael,' she said, touching Alex on the arm as she sat down, 'just wishing us all a Merry Christmas.'

'I thought there might be something wrong,' said Uncle Harry, who had been very quiet through the meal, 'for him to ring at this time.'

Josie put her napkin back on her lap.

'He missed me,' she said simply.

'Love. That's what makes the world go around, doesn't it?' said Daphne.

'Faith,' said BB.

Everyone began talking at once and Alex almost missed his mother leaning over towards Uncle Harry and saying to him as though it were important; 'I'm going home soon. I told Michael.' She had put her hand on the table, not touching Uncle Harry's hand, but just placing it there so that one could imagine that she would touch him if they were alone, and her hand lay on the table, with her bracelet catching the incandescence of the candle flame, like a letter of apology on a silver tray. And at the other end of the table, Aunt Liz had seen it too, but could not have heard the words, because Uncle Bob was talking about television to her in one ear and Mr Doughty was trying to explain to both Daphne and herself about the Building Society in the other. But she had caught the intimacy of the scene and Alex, being sensitive to her unpredictable swings of mood this day, was struck with a feeling of dread as he watched the shadows play over her face as she looked along the table through the flames at her husband and his mother.

Alex looked at the Uncle whom he loved, and he began to be dimly aware of the forces around him, forces and emotions that nobody spoke about. And he knew, in that instant, in the way his mother's hand had lain on the table, and the way Aunt Liz had noticed it, that Aunt Liz was aware of them too. And was aware of them in a way she had not been before, as though whatever she had been keeping at bay over the years with her sharp tongue and brusqueness, had finally, silently, crept under her guard and reached her core, and he wanted to get up and leave the table, run away, but he could not think of a suitable enough excuse to do so and he was stuck to the chair, not just with heat, but with the sheer dread of what he feared would happen.

It was BB of course who opened the sluice gates, by going on about religion and belief, and Aunt Julie, who had been trying to involve her in some conversation about bowling or gardening, two subjects that right at this moment BB was not in the least interested in, threw her hands up in the air and they made shadows on the walls. And although Aunt Liz remained seated, Alex could swear he thought he saw her rear like a venomous spider to attack the nearest victim.

'You!' she spat at BB, and BB looked paralyzed as though the venom from the fangs had indeed reached her. 'You don't believe in anything. You think because you and Josie went to church that you are better than me? Do you think a bit of ritual really makes you a better person or talking about it does? You shed more tears for kittens than you shed for me. You are further away than you've ever been. You're supposed to give witness to belief by the way you act. You don't even know right from wrong!'

'I'm a pragmatic Christian.'

Aunt Liz laughed harshly.

'There's no such thing. It doesn't work that way. You talk about childhood faith. That's all you gave me BB. And you are right about that, it doesn't last, and it doesn't help when you grow up. Does it Josie?'

'Oh, this is horrible,' said Julie pushing away her plate.

'I'll tell you about belief,' said Aunt Liz, pieces of hair escaping from her chignon with each word that poured out. They were all quiet, as though frozen in the path of the oncoming flood. They could see it coming but none of them could avoid it. It was one of those moments when every sound, the clinking of the glasses, the scratch of a fork on the plate, the quickening breeze outside rustling the wisteria, was being listened to by a hundred ears.

'I remember when I was pregnant . . .'

'Liz, for God's sake!' Uncle Harry said sharply.

'There are no family secrets here, Harry. Are there Josie? No family loyalties either. I was so unhappy Josie, when you and Michael were having a baby, and Harry and I were not. How it ate into me. How else was I to prove I was a woman? No, deeper than that. How else was I, a woman, to prove myself?'

Josie ventured softly, 'You had your painting . . .'

'Oh Josie, don't give me that shit. I wanted a baby like everyone else. And I felt somehow, in this house, this place with its traditions,' she almost spat out the word, 'that it was somehow expected of me to produce. To produce anything. But preferably another little Harry. Isn't that right Harry? So I was so happy when old Dr Jones, you remember him, Josie? Julie does, he brought the twins into the world . . .'

'Dr Rollins,' said Julie in a resigned voice, realizing there was no way of avoiding the rush of pain that gushed from Liz, 'his name was Rollins.'

'Yes. Well, old Dr Rollins told me I was pregnant at last. Heavens. This was six or seven years ago. After all those miscarriages and the last tubal pregnancy, I was so happy. I was so careful, taking it easy, nursing it along you know. Until one day Harry insisted on taking me for a ride . . .'

'Liz,' Uncle Harry repeated from his seat at the head of the table, his voice falling like the wax from the candles on the table.

'He wanted to show me the new sheep dip,' she went on, seeing the day before her again in the flame. 'So of course, I couldn't refuse, and of course everything came away. Great clots.'

'Liz.' Harry's head was in his hands.

'We rang Dr Rollins and he said to go straight to bed and while we were waiting for him to come from town, I made a deal.' She looked straight at Alex. Her eyes were wet. 'I made a deal with God. You know I used to paint? I wanted to be an artist once. Well I made a deal with Him. I said that one way or the other, whether I kept the baby or not, I would give up my painting. Stupid, wasn't it? But it was all I could offer him, you see? All I had of worth. I had no other talents. It was my precious bit of gold. Useless bargain. Didn't impress Him a bit. It all came away, my baby. My baby. And that's when Harry began to become interested in this sheep breeding nonsense. All his interest in ovulation. It all stems from then. His little wife was now barren. Right, Harry? The fault is all with me, isn't it? You know that.'

Everyone was so silent, it was unbearable. The lungs crushed against the rib cage screaming for air. Aunt Liz's eyes were brimming, threatening to spill.

At the window a moth battered futilely trying to get in. Alex could hear its soft body thudding against the screen.

Suddenly Uncle Harry slammed his fist down on the table making the dishes rattle. His voice was angry.

'Good God, woman. I've paid. I've paid the price. Lay off will you? Stop putting it all on me. Shoulder some blame yourself. The truth is you can't. You don't want to. You were afraid. You gave up painting because you were afraid you were no good. And you were afraid of finding that out!' He pointed his finger at her along the table. 'You are afraid of failing. Of being human. Failed, flawed humans like the rest of us.'

Aunt Liz began to cry, gutters of tears swept down her cheeks. Alex had never seen an adult cry before, great, gulping, ugly cries that tore at his heart because she made no move to stop them or hide them. Proud Aunt Liz.

'It's not true! It's not true!' she cried.

Julie had risen to go to her when outside there was a sudden and startling clap of thunder which made the family jump and the heavy velvet drapes trembled like living things. There was a second roll, louder than the first, and a huge wind blew the curtains straight out into the room as though they were made of mere paper, and the balloons bounced up and hit the ceiling and one floated free like a sad reminder of some other festive occasion. The whole countryside outside was lit by sheet lightning so that it was as light as day. And then the sky opened up and a deluge of water, torrents of rain, began to pour down over the house and all of Tiddalik.

The frog had laughed.

The noise was deafening as it rattled on the tiles and filled the gutters and rushed down the drainpipes into the water tank. There was so much rain that it sheeted over the edge of the roof and the eaves above the windows and the next searing flash of light came to them through a waterfall outside. Yet it lit the whole room and then the sputtering candles went out, came on, went out again. And the hall lights, all the lights went out. And everything was plunged into darkness.

'Thank God,' said Uncle Bob.

'Thank God for the rain,' said Mr Doughty.

And the Great Frog Tiddalik laughed and laughed.

· TWENTY-ONE ·

'We have to close the windows. The rain is coming in.' Aunt Liz's voice, still racked with sobs, came through the noise of the deluge.

They all got up and went in different directions, stumbling through the dark to close windows and doors, upstairs and throughout the house. Alex went to the bay windows to help Aunt Liz shut out the elements. The windows were stuck, swollen in the old wooden frames, and it took both of them all their strength to pull them down. They were very wet when they finally closed them.

Cynthia came in with extra candles, the electricity going off being a normal occurrence in violent storms. What they never knew, though, was how long it would take to come back on. Cynthia lit the candles on the table and Daphne was the only one still sitting there, surrounded by the remains of chewed turkey legs and abandoned napkins and paper hats and torn bon-bons. She kept shaking her head as though trying to clear her vision.

'I'm just about to give up, back there,' said Cynthia, putting her hands on her hips and then changing her mind and rubbing her lower back.

'You're doing a fine job, Cynthia,' said Uncle Harry, coming back into the room. 'Here, have a drink.' He poured a glass of wine for Cynthia and then poured himself one and drank it down. The others were drifting back and Julie directed the girls to clear the table with Cynthia. Aunt Liz stood desolate in her dark red frock with the stains of the rain making wrinkled blotches where before all had been smooth. Alex's mother came in with Mr Doughty, and took her seat. She looked as miserable as Alex felt. And BB scuttled in with Bob, keeping her back to the wall, as though she had to protect it. The girls wheeled out the trolley making an horrendous squeaking job about it, but nobody said anything. The rain drummed down on the house, blotting out all other sounds. Bob went around and filled everyone's glasses again. The twins came back and said Cynthia said, if someone didn't come and hold a flashlight for her while she lifted the Christmas pudding out of the boiling water, she was going to have an accident. And she wouldn't let them help because she thought they might get scalded.

'I'll go,' said Mr Doughty, only too happy to leave the table. Julie put two jugs of hard sauce on the table and Uncle Harry, for want of something to do, took some matches out of his pocket and lit the candles on the mantelpiece again.

Aunt Liz went over to him. She walked as someone going to a scaffold.

'I'm sorry,' she said.

Uncle Bob got hastily to his feet, scraping his chair on the floor.

'I'll just go and get another bottle of champers from the 'fridge,' he said. He hitched up his trousers with his good hand and shot out of the room to join Mr Doughty.

Liz and Harry were at the mantelpiece behind BB.

Aunt Liz turned around into the room and said;

'I'm really sorry for going off the deep end like that.'

No one said anything, and behind BB's head Uncle Harry lifted his hand and touched a wrinkled stain on the shoulder of Liz's dress. It was the merest touch, over in a slow instant, but it seemed to young Alex watching, that the touch conveyed words, I am sorry too, which his Aunt accepted by standing for the briefest moment, before she turned away and went back to her chair.

Alex began to wonder whether he too should leave the room, when BB found her voice and said;

'I am very glad you apologized, Liz. And I accept, though I really don't know why I should. You were very rude — disparaging me and everything. And if I did bring you up so badly, how come you've turned out so well? You're so perfect. You say you don't believe in God any more, how come you're the only one here that's made a deal with Him — and stuck to it.' Her eyes narrowed.

'Anyway you make too much of this painting thing if you ask me . . .'

'I didn't.'

'Let me tell you,' BB went on, to no-one in particular, 'Liz once painted a portrait of me. A portrait! Hah! I had a face like a landscape. My eyes were bushes, my nose was a rivulet running into my mouth, my cheeks were hills. It was horrible. Horrible. Furrows were gouged across my forehead. You are not a portraitist, Liz, if you don't mind me saying so . . .'

'You'd be surprised,' Aunt Liz said.

'. . . but I accept your apology.'

'I wasn't really apologizing to you, BB,' Aunt Liz said in a tired voice, as though she had travelled a thousand miles, 'I was apologizing to Alex.'

Alex looked at her, but BB's voice cut across their communication like a razor through soft butter.

'Alex. Alex. I'm sick of Alex. Whose boy is he anyway?'

The world, for Alex, turned upside down. He saw BB's hand fly to her mouth, her lips trying to eat her knuckles. Great Granny Daphne's cane rattled to the floor as she tried to rise.

But Alex's attention was on his mother. She had jumped up and run around the table before anyone could stop her. She had her hands on BB's throat and was shaking her so violently that Alex thought BB's small head would snap and roll off. He could hear BB gurgling in her throat. He was listening to his mother, her voice reaching him in snatches, sounding like a mad woman, over the sound of the incessant rain.

'You bitch. You bitch. I'll kill you for that.'

In the candlelight he could see Uncle Harry trying to pull her away from BB. Uncle Harry had his hands in his mother's thick hair trying to yank her back. Aunt Liz, was it Aunt Liz? pulling at BB, her arms around her waist. Daphne was pounding her stick into the floor shouting, 'No, No, No.' His mother's voice had reached a scream, but he could only hear the echo of BB's words, 'Whose boy is he anyway?' and the words were beating into his skull as loud as the rain beating onto the roof. Hammering, hammering at him. This was a nightmare, he was dreaming this in some strange place where everything was upside down, an *Alice Through the Looking Glass* adventure in which, instead of everything being too small, everything was too big, too large to encompass. His mother, his aunt, his uncle and his grandmother, shouting at each other, struggling, all caught in a drama which concerned him. Which they knew. They knew! Alex tried to shut the sounds out of his head. He put his hands over his ears.

'Stop it! Stop it!' he screamed. They heard him. They stopped. They turned around and looked at him. He could see their faces but he did not recognize them. He was in a cavern, somewhere strange and mysterious, where mythical creatures lurked to grasp him if he strayed. Where was this? This place of flickering lights and oriental barques, green water streaming down and shadows of haunting shapes changing on the walls? If he touched the walls he knew they would be soft and spongy, cold, damp, pitted to the touch. He backed out of the room.

'Alex. Alex,' someone shouted. That was not him? Whose boy was he anyway? Who was he? He ran into the dark hall. Girls screamed. He could see a circle of blue flame approaching him from the other end of the hall. Cynthia, another secret, was advancing with the pudding. Alex ran past her. He knocked the flaming, brandied pudding out of her hands.

'Oh, bugger it, I've had it!' she said.

'Hey! I say old boy.'

'Bloody hell. What's going on?'

'Alex! Alex!'

He was out of the door, onto the verandah, down the steps. He was in the rain. A wonderful, drenching coolness, wetness running into his eyes, plastering down his hair, rain running down his face so the tears did not taste so salty on his lips. Running, stumbling in the dark, in the teeming sheets of water, mud underfoot, tripping over roots and branches, crossing a fence, until he came to a high point where there was nothing. Nothing but an obelisk: a cool marble surface he could put his face against and sob and cry and kick where no-one could see or hear him.

'Oh, I hate Christmas,' he sobbed. 'I hate this place.'

Alex lost track of time, up on the little hill where his grandfather was buried. But he knew some time had passed because the rain had steadied down now to a comfortable patter. His heart had stopped pounding and his breathing was easier. No lights had gone on in the Big House. He would have seen them if they had. He saw the headlights of the truck coming out and up the hill towards him. Someone with a flashlight got out. The flashlight swung around, there were faint voices, were they calling him? He couldn't be sure. The truck went away and he saw a dim glow in a window nearby; Cynthia had been brought home. He was very close to her house, he realized.

He sat on the slab leaning against the obelisk feeling quite safe up here. He was not sure what he felt safe from. In the dark, his fingers felt the engraved letters in the smooth marble. He could make out an L, a B, an O, L O V I N G, he couldn't make out the rest. He guessed he was at Uncle Harry's family vault. He would not have come here voluntarily he knew. He saw the pale gleam of candlelight from Cynthia's window. It reassured him. He thought about Cynthia and her big belly. And he thought about his mother and his aunt and Uncle Harry. He did not know what the trouble was between them, but he guessed that Uncle Harry loved his mother. Must once have loved his mother. And that Aunt Liz knew about it, which explained her behaviour. And Uncle Harry loved Aunt Liz too. He could see that. He thought about it, and he knew that what BB was alluding to was this. And the question which had upset them all was about his father. Or who his father was.

He thought about his father and his mother. But he couldn't fathom adult emotions. He could only guess at the passion and depth of them. Could only guess what had happened before he was born, or since. He didn't know who his father was. Perhaps it was Uncle Harry. Only his mother knew for sure. But there was one thing he *did* know. None of them loved BB. Certainly not him. He hated her.

Just as he was thinking of her, he saw another flashlight coming the same way as the truck had, up to Cynthia's cottage. He waited tensely, watching its quavering progress in the rain. Then he heard BB's voice. Calling him. He drew back against the obelisk terrified of being seen. The flashlight paused, then it went towards Cynthia's house. It went out. He could hear voices. He could hear Cynthia's voice raised. And then the flashlight, having been doused, came on again and went away. Then Alex heard a scream. He listened again. It was Cynthia, he could swear. It was coming from her house. He could see the flashlight still wobbling away down into the yards. She must have heard. She must have heard.

Alex ran down to Cynthia's house. He fell once or twice but picked himself up. He fumbled at the door, impatient to find the latch and then went in. He could hear Cynthia groaning from the bedroom. He hesitated.

'Cynthia? Cynthia?' He groped his way across the room.

'Oh, help me. Help me please.' He couldn't see a thing. There was one small candle on the dresser. He went towards the bed, felt her on the floor, knelt down.

She clutched his wet blazer, recognized his voice.

'Oh Alex, Alex. Help me. It's the baby. It's coming.'

'I'll go and get help.'

'No, please don't leave me. It's nearly here. It's just the pain. Like waves,' she gripped his hand so tightly that he knew he could not leave. 'I'm going under,' she screamed again. When the wave receded she said, 'I've been feeling crook all day, and my back aching. But I've felt that before. I thought I had more time. Oh Alex.'

'I need some light. Some light.'

'Don't let go my hand.'

'Just to get the candle. Let me go. Just for a minute.'

He brought the candle over. He could see her poor, wet, face, drenched with perspiration. He saw the fear and the youth on it. She was not much older than he was. He pulled the sheets and pillows off the bed and stuffed them behind her and under her. Cynthia was sobbing between her pains.

'I wish Jim was here. He's probably gone and got drunk again. Afraid he is. Afraid of this little baby coming that's his. Isn't it stupid to be afraid of the one thing that's going to bring you happiness?'

He wiped her face with a corner of the sheet. He was so afraid himself. 'Yes. Yes,' he said.

'Jim was supposed to be here. He promised he would be here tonight.' A shuddering contraction went through her. She moaned. 'Oh God. When will it stop?'

Alex didn't know what else he could do to help her. He had watched Uncle Harry and Reilley deliver twin lambs and that was all.

'Why didn't BB stay? I saw her coming up to the house.'

'She wouldn't help me. She wouldn't help! She was looking for you, Alex. She said she didn't want to bring no black bastard into the world.'

Another wrenching pain sent Cynthia down into the trough of the waves.

'Can you see it, can you see it yet?'

Alex thought of Uncle Harry. 'Now young Alex, keep your wits about you.' Alex moved the candle. He used the sheet to wipe the blood and water away. In the dim light he thought he could just make out the top of the baby's head.

'It's nearly here, Cynthia, it's nearly here. If you just push a bit, push a bit more.' He was sweating as much as Cynthia and he began to cry again himself, wiping the blood that was trickling down her legs, looking at the spreading stains on the sheet and thinking they would never wash out. And all he could do was whisper to her that it was all right, that she was doing fine, for he couldn't let her see the fear in his eyes having caught sight of her own. And he prayed to God to let the baby come, please come, and he prayed to his Grandmother's St Antony, and he prayed to Cynthia's Dad to put in a good word with the Spirits on his Great Walkabout. And somebody listened, for with a last painful contraction and a shuddering cry from Cynthia, the baby's head was out.

'Another push, another push Cynthia.'

Alex had hold of the baby's head now, holding it so gently with his hands, the hair thick and covered with a whitish wax. 'Oh Cynthia,' he said and first one shoulder, then the other, slipped out. The tiny hands were out grasping at the air, struggling for life, already wanting to grab hold. Alex turned the baby over as it slipped into the world. Like a little rabbit it felt, he remembered, but oh, so much more.

'Look Cynthia, look.'

She raised her head and saw the whole body of her little son rising out of her own. Alex placed the baby, her warm, living extension, the umbilical cord still attached, on her stomach. Cynthia put her finger in the baby's mouth to clear it. The baby began to cry. The placenta came out in a big heap. Alex covered Cynthia and the baby with the candlewick bed cover.

'Oh, oh,' said Cynthia holding her baby to her. Alex touched the baby's hand in wonder. The little fingers grasped at his. He had never felt anything so beautiful.

'Will you be all right now, while I run and get some help?'

Cynthia didn't take her eyes from the baby, examining his ears, his toes, his tiny fingers.

'*You* be all right, little man. I'll kill that bitch if she gets hold of you.' Her eyes were luminous in the candlelight. 'Go and get help now. But you already done all the work.'

Alex's feet flew over the ground. It was still black outside. Black as the baby. He laughed out aloud in the soft rain. He was exhilarated. He had brought someone into the world. He had been able to help. He was not a boy any more, useless to everyone. Not a baby like the one he had just delivered. Like he had been once.

Cynthia, the mother. Just as his mother had given birth to him. She had felt the same pains, sweated and cried to bring him into the world. He would always be his mother's child, no matter how old he grew. No matter where he went in this world. Or the next. He was her son. Her boy. BB's question was no longer of importance to him. It was meaningless. One day his mother would explain it to him. For him, now, that was enough.

He ran through the gate to the garden, leaving it swinging open behind him. The rain was spattering down now very lightly. The storm was over. And as he reached the back door of the Big House, the lights came back on and the generator roared back into action and he saw his uncle, and his mother, and his aunt, all standing in the hall, their faces worried and their clothes soaked from searching for him. And he felt surrounded by love because of their anxiety. But he waved aside their questions. He was full of his own answers, his own light.

'Come quick. Come quick,' he shouted. 'Get the car, Uncle Harry. Cynthia's had her baby!'

· TWENTY-TWO ·

She was awake before dawn. She lay there listening, in her own bed, in her again empty house, to the 'possum which had woken her. She could hear the scrabbling of its feet, the brush of its tail overhead. She threw her slipper up once, ineffectually, at the ceiling.

But she could not get back to sleep. Her mind was red-hot. It was a sensation she recognized from other days. She met it, not exactly as a friend, more as an aquaintance with whom she was on nodding terms. But never before had the sensation arrived with such intensity, an intensity with which, when she opened her eyes, even the eyeballs saw red embers in front of them. It was like the colour abstraction of a certainty. This is it. This is what I have been waiting for. But wait a minute, another part of her said: the cool blue line between this red-hot reality and herself, this said, what are you talking about? She closed her eyes and opened them again and she could see and she turned her head and looked out through the open curtain at the washed dawn sky reflecting the colours she felt.

She saw the sun, heaving itself up for another day, burning up, orange, pouring itself across the sky to paint in ochres and reds the wisps of clouds fleeing the night.

They had all fled in the night; the clouds, the people. What a fiasco. But she was indifferent to the sequence of events, had put a distance between herself and that terrible table, that awful moment when Josie had put her hands around her throat, had called her all those filthy names. Bitch. Whore. If, BB thought, swinging her legs blindly over the side of the bed and sitting up, if only Josie had given her a chance. To explain. That she had meant no harm. It had just slipped out. She rubbed her bruised neck. Her timing had never been right. But then, neither had Daphne's nor her daughters'.

BB padded into the kitchen. She stood dreaming for a moment in the middle of the small space. She heard a tiny scurrying sound, and then a snap behind the refrigerator. Caught the bugger at last, she thought. But she was not elated as she normally would have been, was instead, incurious. BB thought of the many traps she had been caught in and her struggles to escape them when she realized what they were. She took a glass of water from the tap and drank it greedily letting it dribble down her chin.

BB walked distractedly into the dim sitting room, standing looking at the boxes and the sewing machine, the glass fronted thingamajig. All her memories were here, all her life. The bits she had shared with the girls, the bits she had shared with their father. It was not that he'd been a bad man. She had realized that after she left him. But he hadn't fulfilled the promise she felt life had made to her. And when she had tried to wrest her life back to herself, she only made it worse. That madness when the girls were young, when her body had been in the red heat her mind was in now, seemed as though it had happened to someone else. BB held the empty water glass against her shrunken stomach. She felt the bottom of the glass against her pubic bone. How full of juice she once had been.

BB put down her glass on the sewing machine and went back into her room. She pulled on the dress she had worn last night, she did not care that it was crumpled and dirty. Put on her sandals with the thong through the toes. It was going to be another hot day. The walls of her little house felt tinder dry despite the rain of the night before. The rain had washed over it, running down the grooves of the corrugated iron roof and out onto the splayed roof of the verandah and into the water tank at the side. Never touched the wooden frame, thought BB, feeling the heat radiating towards her. She wished her body had been like that.

BB was insensible to hunger this morning. There was no Daphne to look after now. Her eyes squeezed out a warm tear of self-pity as she stepped onto her verandah and saw the shards of the clay pots still lying there where she had swept them to one side. There were some sheets of paper blowing about, neatly filled in with handwritten data. She couldn't think what they were or how they had got there, until she stepped on one in a steaming puddle and saw *Breeding Ewes* written on it. And she remembered how last night she had hidden in Harry's office for a while hoping to catch young Alex. Was that after or before she had gone up to Cynthia's house? After. She had gone to Cynthia's first after skulking about outside the Big House. She had run away from the dining room when all their attention was diverted by Alex. She was angry and Cynthia had been crying that the baby was coming. And BB had thought about how she had suffered to bring her own daughters into this world, and had they appreciated it? No, not a damn bit. She remembered how she had sat pricking her fingers sewing for them when they were children while outside the Harbour beckoned. She hadn't always given in.

Last night all she wanted to do was sprinkle Alex with a bit of water for heaven's sake. But she hadn't found him and hiding in Harry's office she had seen with her flashlight, the charts on the wall. She had taken them down, not sure what she would do with them, or even what they were, but saw in them another way to get even, if all else failed. She was angry with all of them by then. And she had torn some pages off, just as once in a rage she had ripped the lace trim off her Italian Mama's petticoat. And then walking up the hill in the rain, she had fallen and lost some other pages, and she searched now with her eyes, and saw a few, crumpled, sodden, so they looked like white cockatoos feeding on the grass. She had been so distressed last night, she thought now stepping down the rutted road and then changing her mind and going towards the river, it's not every day that someone tries to kill you.

She would take a boat ride. She would probably never get to take Alex on the river now. They would all keep him away from her. The paddocks she crossed were little changed by the rain. The narrow sheep paths on the slope had mud tracks on them and the grass at the side looked as though it had been dragged with a wide-toothed comb. Already the mud was drying and cracking in the sun.

Brown, brown land, she thought as she walked. When she had first come to Australia, how she had disliked it, the sameness of it, the emptiness of it. It had seemed to her an indifferent place, indifferent to people who came, who lived and breathed and loved and hated and died on it. It had always been so, Liz had said, but BB took it as a personal affront. 'Love it the way it is,' said Liz. But BB hadn't listened, instead had thrown gallons of water over her patch of a garden, had seeds and plants from nurseries in Melbourne and Sydney sent to her, to fight it. And the minute her back was turned, they all died, and it was brown again instead of green. The land had won, and it didn't care. Liz had been right. Again. BB popped her knuckles as she walked towards the boat. Liz was always right, that was the rub. How could she have produced so irritating a daughter?

BB came to the river, running today brown and ugly and swollen, bubbling with a dirty cream foam on its surface. The boat was there and she got in and untethered it from a tea-tree bush and it swung away into the current. She put her arm out once into the foam, just to see if the foam would crack, but it was disappointingly insubstantial. She should have known. BB pulled her arm in. She let the river take her where it wanted, just as most of her life she had let rivers swirl her along. BB stayed in the boat for hours allowing herself to be bumped against the side, into sand banks, giddily turning in midstream only to be caught in the arms of some partly submerged tree. But gradually the river dwindled to a stream, the boat stuck fast and after waiting an interminable time for something to happen, BB sat up and saw that the boat had run out of water.

BB got out and began walking back the way she had come. She was a long way down the river, way past the shearing sheds and the river flats where once Harry had grown a lucerne crop. The sun was high overhead and she knew it would be a long walk back. No one would come looking for her. No one. They would not miss her. But she didn't care. She had tried to save Alex's soul, that was all. She stopped and took a bottle from the pocket of her dress. It had been there since last night. She took the cork out with her teeth and poured the water into the river. She watched the pale trickle run into the brown. What a blessing it might have been. One thing she had tried to do. And again: useless.

It took BB ages to get back to her house. She was very thirsty. She should have drunk the holy water she thought, except she knew that she never could. She could see her house shimmering in the heat, sitting on its hill. There was a blister between her big toe and the next. If only she could walk a few more paces, get inside and sit in the cool. Even her hot little house would feel like an ice palace after this. It must be two, three, four o'clock. BB felt dizzy from lack of food. Up the hill, over the fence, skirt torn, leg bleeding, geraniums, oh poor geraniums, the give of the sagging floors of the verandah. She stepped inside the blissful darkness of her house, went to the kitchen and drank straight from the tap, splashing her face and neck with water. She sat on the cool linoleum floor with her skirt up until the dizziness passed and

when she felt better she got up and put on the kettle for a
cup of tea, pushing aside the dishes and cloths from yesterday
and the recipe clippings and a pan of rancid mutton dripping.
And then BB staggered into her bedroom and lay down amidst
the photographs and the letters and the orange peel on her
bed and listened for the kettle to boil. And the house was so
quiet she could hear the feathers in her pillow breaking under
her head. She felt so lonely and sorry for herself that tears
gushed out of her eyes.

She had a good mind to show them all, to finish herself
off and then see how they would feel. Guilty. She could write
a note absolving them of blame, that would turn the screw.
She could have a sherry and swallow something, ammonia
perhaps, or rat poison, she couldn't do it with something
hard and nasty like a knife. BB pressed her nails hard into
her wrist. No, she couldn't cut herself. Once, as a child she
had tried to show her mother that she didn't need her. She
had scraped all the heads off a box of matches, but it took
too long and she had got bored. So she had run away instead.
She only got as far as the sweet pea nursery at the corner of
the main road, where she sat until it got dark and the seductive
perfume of the flowers told her to go home.

Slipping now into exhausted half-sleep, timing her breathing to the 'possum's upstairs, BB could no longer keep her
memories at bay. They crowded around. She heard her Papa
whistle. He used to whistle themes from Puccini for her
because he couldn't sing in key. In the haze, in the red twilight,
BB could see him at the end of her bed. He had a pencil stuck
behind his ear. He had come for a visit and brought Mama
with him. Mama hadn't changed. She still had the wen under
her chin that she once told BB was the tail of a cat she had
swallowed. Mama wiped her brow. It was hot in here. BB
felt the heat licking at her. There were other people in the
room. A funny little soldier with a moustache, vaguely familiar, who stroked her toes as he went past. How did he know

she liked that? And here was Josie with her arms around Alex as though protecting him. They were followed by Liz, Liz walking with her arms out, playing Portia no doubt, and hoisting herself up onto the dressing table where she sat leaning against the mirror with her arms folded. The haze had turned to smoke. Through her smarting eyes BB saw Liz's father in a brown suit and he was holding Daphne's hand. Liz jumped down and ran to the door and shouted but the words came out as a tunnel, the letters forming a vortex into which BB was being sucked.

She tried to grip the sides of the bed to stop the headlong rush. But the red heat had hold of her. It had been waiting for her all day. And now it embraced her like a lover promising eternal fidelity and care. The fire swept past her and reached her boxes and roared, licked and caught, like the tongue of a salamander, the lengths of old material, the skeins of bargain basement wool, the foam pieces for pillows.

BB fell to the floor, while the flames ate her precious things, her own tarnished bits of gold. The curtains lit, and now the wall between her room and the next was gone and through the gap she could see the fingers of flame lifting the spread on the sewing machine, tossing it, playing with it. Oh, she'd made that once, don't do that. Sewn it by hand on the ship coming to Australia, when Liz was already quickening with life inside her.

But the fire was in control. And now all that was left was a singed photograph, a crinkled square lying beside her eye. Babies. Josie and Liz with her, taken long ago. A perfect moment caught in black and white. Trying to understand, BB reached for it but it melted in her hand. And then there was nothing.

· TWENTY-THREE ·

It was the afternoon of the funeral and once the mourners had left, Liz and Josie sat on the verandah of the Big House in the sun. In their dark coloured clothes, they looked like moths that had strayed from their usual habitat.

It was a particularly beautiful day, a day on which the countryside opens its arms and says 'Lie down beside me'. The intense heat of the week before had gone and a small breeze lifted the fronds of the wisteria and shook the heavy blooms against the verandah posts. Even the flies were absent and the walk behind the bearers up to the family vault had been a pleasant stroll through the short bristling grass with the songs of the butcherbirds and magpies accompanying them.

There had not been much left to bury and the funeral director had originally suggested cremation, but Liz told him BB was a Catholic, and because she had made no arrangements for her own plot, the Barton family vault had been opened up. There was plenty of room, Harry said. A small dusty band of mourners, their cars following the hearse after the service in town, bumped along the roads to Tiddalik. The cars and the hearse had parked in the circle in front of the stables and they had walked sombrely, but without tears, through the yards and up past Cynthia's cottage to the vault, and listened to Father Murphy's words; words which seemed to have as little bearing on the woman they knew as the marble obelisk had to the dusty ground from which it rose.

And afterwards, in the darkened dining room, while they had tea and scones and ate the shortbread that Julie had thoughtfully brought with her, they had all tried to say kind and truthful things about BB, which was more difficult for some than others. People soon slipped away. Daphne off to Mr Doughty's house where she felt, she said, quite at home: Mr Doughty had a cat. And Mr Doughty, who had after all been married to the same woman for forty-nine years, and had found on her death that his life in fact had not been as independent as she had led him to imagine, wanted to replace this pivot to his household. He was glad to have Daphne in his home he said to the girls on departing in his little blue car, for he was tired of 'listening to rooms echoing without words'. Liz watched them drive away, Daphne overflowing the bucket seat in front, and wondered whether faults were not like cogs that kept people together.

A small bird darted in under the eave of the house and disappeared into a tiny hole near a pipe on the wall. Josie moved in her chair and a drift of eau de Cologne carried by the soft breeze came between her and Liz. It hung in the air like all the unspoken, forbidden thoughts that were never far from their minds.

The scent of Josie; it had been in Harry's hair, faintly on his skin. It had come to her in the night, on Christmas Eve, that whiff of her sister's distinctive perfume, when Harry had touched her in his sleep and she had come up out of a dream trying to grasp some detail that was strange but familiar. Was it a sound that had woken her? Ruby sleeping in the hall? No more Ruby. Was it Daphne, calling out in some nightmare? She had listened. No, not Daphne. Daphne was asleep in the Milky Way searching for Porry. Liz had turned over. But then she did hear a sound. She heard the stairs creaking as Josie came home from church, heard her quietly push open a door, heard the faint murmur of voices. Josie with her son. Josie.

Josie. Josie's perfume. Josie with Harry. Liz recoiled from Harry's hand. They had been together. Oh, she knew it without a doubt. And the pain in her was so palpable that she put her hand on her heart. It felt constricted like her throat. Her own pride, her own egoism, that they could destroy it so easily. Couldn't they see how it diminished her, not only in their eyes, but in her own? Liz had rolled to the far side of the great bed, as far away from Harry as she could. She had curled up around her own misery.

She had not cried that night, not got up, not made a scene. Only on Christmas morning, seeing her own distraught face in the bathroom mirror, like a child seeing blood from a cut and bursting into tears, did the betrayal hit her. What have they done to me? And then, sitting beside the Christmas tree, the lights winking on and off, her toast and tea beside her on the floor, she had opened Harry's present to her, touched the rich, silk, embroidered kimono with its chrysanthemums. A perfect gift for her, which only he could give, because only he knew the sensuous interior that was her, the thick tender moon of the artichoke which was her, which could only be eaten when the thistles were pulled aside. But what use, what use was a sign of love, if the real thing was missing? For years she had pushed under the resentment, the anger, the fear, had smothered the nub of what she knew with layers of self-sufficiency. But like a stubborn seed it had grown and had appeared, a flourishing weed, in the desert of her dining table. She had tried to kill it but BB had nourished it, watered it, and finally blown away the last grains of sand that hid it from view.

And after that one satisfying, agonizing outburst at the table, Liz had immediately regretted it. Because, if everything were stripped bare, exposed, left pitilessly without water, like this land she loved, everything would die. Even love died if not cared for.

She was looking at the white trunks of the ghost gums,

the stunted kurrajongs along the drive, the stringybark trees further down where the garden petered out and the river paddocks began. She could see Alex down there practising with his stock whip. She did not know where Harry was. She felt colourless and heavy. 'I hate those trees,' she said, 'those stringybarks. They are so untidy, such a dead, grey, brown colour.'

'Yes.'

'I can't believe she's gone. And to go so horribly. Christ, I wouldn't wish that on anybody.' She blew her nose. 'I miss her. Who would have thought that was possible? Me with my big sharp tongue, always using it to lash her. If only she had let me be. Is it so hard to let a daughter be? All I wanted from her was . . . love. She never could give it to me. Oh God, if only we could go back and undo things. But we never can. Why couldn't she accept me the way I was? I always disappointed her. She wanted me to be like you. Always like you, the pretty one. The one who made no trouble. Oh Christ.'

'Don't cry, please.'

'Every day of my life seems to have been spent thinking of BB, fighting with BB. Now I feel cleaned out. Scraped.'

'I do too.'

'That morning, Boxing Day, when the phone rang it made me jump. I was in a deep sleep. Harry answered it. It was the police station. I thought it must be about BB. I had this terrible premonition about her reaction to . . . to us. But it was about Jim, in jail for being drunk and disorderly.'

'Surprise, surprise.'

'. . . And could Harry come and bail him out? There was some damage we had to pay for too. He'd thrown a brick through the grog shop window and broken a street light, driving into it when he tried to come home.'

'He didn't look too good at the hospital that morning.'

'No. Harry tried to clean him up in the men's room before

taking him in to see Cynthia. But Cynthia said he still looked like death and he stank of booze.'

'What did he say about his son?'

'He was too angry and bemused to speak a straight sentence. He came storming out of the ward with the blackest look on his face. He and Cynthia and Daphne had had a good old hate session about BB before we arrived.'

'Well, we all had those.'

'And Harry was in a terrible mood. BB stole his charts, that's all we can think. He found torn pieces and the clipboard up near her house. Why would she do such a thing? Years of work gone. He can never replace them. Destroyed. For what? For *what*?' Liz sat looking out across the paddocks. Alex was still down there with his stock whip and at last he managed to snap it so that it gave a loud crack.

Josie stood up to get a better view of her son.

'I don't have any answers, not any more,' she said, holding on to the rough warm stone balustrade. 'I don't think there are any. Do I sound like you now, Liz?' She turned to look at her sister. Liz's cat had jumped up and was sitting shedding hairs on to her dark skirt. She watched the cat groom itself while Liz played absently with its ears.

'I don't think I am like you, really,' Josie said softly. 'I wish I was,' she whispered, but the words were like a breath lost in the perfume of the flowering wisteria. 'I'm like BB. I've been trying to pretend I'm not. But it's true.

'I was in the country one night, in upstate New York. Michael was in the city and Alex was asleep upstairs. It was very quiet and dark and I was sitting facing the window typing. I was trying to write a love poem,' she laughed gently at herself. 'And I looked up at the window and BB was there. And her face for once was not perplexed, just a face, like you see on the subway or at a lunch counter, a bit tired as though she had just looked up from her sewing and her thoughts were a million miles away. And I thought, what is she doing here? And then I realized of course. It was me. My own image staring back at me.' She pulled an unopened bloom off the vine and ran it over her cheek.

Liz went on stroking her cat. Alex's stock whip cracked again.

'I'll never forget the sight of that smoke curling up above Tiddalik. Could we have stopped it if we'd arrived sooner?'

'I doubt it,' said Liz, 'Jim was here picking up some extra clothes for Cynthia and he hadn't seen a thing until we arrived and Harry shouted at him to get the truck up there fast. I can't understand how he didn't see it. Or smell it.' Liz shook her head.

'Alex was here too, and he didn't see anything either until it was too late. He did so want to come in and see Cynthia and the baby. She's going to call it Alexander you know.'

'Alexander Wariapendi Partridge. Wariapendi. Cynthia took it from a Mary Gilmore poem. It means "looking for something". It would have suited BB.' Liz put her head back and recited from memory with her eyes closed;

'Mark, O Churinga-land,
Where in the dusk stands a dim shadow!
Soon thou shalt seek and not find it –
Thou who has driven Arunta outward,
Sent Arunta crying,
Wariapendi, to Biami,
Wariapendi, to the last.'

'No. It wouldn't have made any difference who had been here. Poor Alex. I kept telling that damn sister that he had delivered the damn baby for heaven's sake. But she wouldn't budge. No children under fourteen allowed to visit. Remember when we were kids and they wouldn't let us visit Dad. No, our being here wouldn't have made any difference.'

The smoke had been pouring from BB's house that early evening, rising high into the air. As they got closer, they could

233

see the flames licking out the windows, curling up under the eaves, then shooting straight up into the sky. It seemed as though the interior of the little house was lit up, each window bursting with orange light. Harry was already there standing helplessly with a bucket in his hand watching the inferno. Jim was driving up the track behind them, with the truck and the water tank. Too late.

'Too late. Too late,' said Liz sitting on the verandah, gazing at the skyline and the blackened stack of BB's chimney.

'Nobody could have stopped it, once it had gone so far. Stupid, careless old woman. It started in the kitchen they reckon. Why wouldn't she clean it up? I told her again and again what a hazard that house was.'

Josie and Liz sat together on the verandah thinking about the past. It was Josie, her fingers clasped around her knees, who looked to the future first.

'I called the airline this morning. I'm leaving tomorrow.' She paused. 'I shouldn't have come.'

Liz said nothing for a long time, then turned to her sister.

'Will you ever bring Alex again?'

Liz and Josie looked into each other's eyes, so alike, so different.

'No. I don't think so.'

Liz stood up, smoothing her skirt with her hands.

'Well, that's that then, isn't it?' She put one hand on her hip, the other up to shade her eyes and looked up the hill to BB's chimney where it stood black and solitary against the blue sky. After a while, Liz knew, it would appear to be just another tree on the skyline. It would crumble down, disintegrate, become grey and old, indecipherable from the other trees and rocks. And there would come a time, she knew, when she would look out and she wouldn't see it any more. But her mind would pinpoint its position exactly, because the chimney stack, and what it stood for, could never be erased from her memory.

'So it is all over,' she said.

Josie said nothing. She was watching her son coming up the hill towards the house, coiling his stock whip in his hand. She could see the way he moved, the smile on his face under the broad-brimmed hat, how like Harry he was. And she wished with her whole heart that her mother BB could have had this grace; the knowledge really to see what was around her, to treasure a minute like this when a mother saw her child safe, with the sun on him, oblivious to her watching, but coming towards her and she with this ache inside that would never go away. And watching Alex she saw him make a movement with his arm that was so like one of her own that she smiled. Because now she could only see herself in him. And then he made a face, which was neither hers nor Harry's, not even borrowed from Michael. But was his own. And she could allow him that too.

'Yes. It is all over,' she said.

Josie put out her hand as though she wanted to hold something. For a moment Liz thought Josie was going to touch her, and she froze. But she had misunderstood the gesture for Josie allowed her hand to drop and turned and faced her sister silently. And in the dropping of her hand she said, I give him up. And Liz acknowledged nothing. There was nothing more to say. Josie went around her sister and into the house. Liz stood looking out at the paddocks, empty now in front of the house, and waited to hear the fly screen door close, but Josie closed it so softly behind her that it sounded merely like a sigh on a quiet afternoon.

· TWENTY-FOUR ·

They were gone.

The whole of Tiddalik was empty of people except for Harry and Liz.

'Do you want rissoles for supper?'

It was late, they were eating quietly in the kitchen, only the ticking of the clock towards midnight and the New Year competed with the click of their spoons and knives. It was a soft, soft night. The guests' sheets were laundered and back in the linen cupboard. In the drawing room, the Christmas tree was dropping pine needles on the floor.

They were wary of each other, as people are who have been separated for a long time. She had locked him out of her room the past few nights, unable to bear the dishonesty of his body beside her in the bed. Even with understanding, forgiveness took time.

She had not wanted him with her, yet she knew that when he did come, her body would dissolve for him. She had lain rigid when she heard him try the door handle last night. It was the first time he had come to the door. He did not call out, only rattled the handle once or twice and then she had heard his footsteps going along the hall and she had discovered in the morning that he had slept in the room Alex had been in. Without sheets. The thought of the hot blankets on him solaced her small revenge.

He had told her that he had paid Jim off, that Jim and Cynthia had to be off the place. This was Saturday, right after

Josie and Alex had left. They had driven into town and said goodbye at the airport terminal bus. Harry and Alex had clung to each other. The women had stood back.

When they returned, Harry had gone immediately into his office and shut the door behind him. He wanted to be alone with his despair. He would never achieve his dreams now, never see his name in the history books beside that of Professor Robinson. There were others who would have the data, would receive some of the accolades. Not him. Liz had wandered back to her house, her house again. All to herself. There was time to do small things, to pick a grapefruit from the tree, to sit and touch the stone walls behind her, feel the little shells with her fingers, warm under the sun. So she did. She sat and peeled one of her grapefruits and ate it, and watched the magpies attacking the unripe plums in the fruit trees, and waited for Harry to come out of his office, to cross the dusty circle, to come through the gate, into the garden, to their house. She saw Jim go into the office.

Jim spoke first;

'Boss . . .'

'I don't want to hear your bloody excuses, Jim. I want you off the place.'

He was writing out a cheque. He would not look up and see Jim's face. 'BB burned to death and you let it happen. What were you doing? Having a quick drink?'

'Boss, you been like a son to me,' said Jim, twirling his hat nervously in his fingers. 'And I got to tell you so you don't go thinking bad about me the rest of your life.'

Jim began to blubber. 'You got to listen Boss. I swear, I didn't see the fire. Honest, not until it was too late, and you came back.' Harry's face was stony. Jim shouted at him, 'Well it would have deserved her if I did. She didn't help Cyn when she needed help. God, any decent person would have stayed and helped the girl. But she? No. Not her, the bitch. I should have known. Because I knew her once. When she was a barmaid in Sydney. Yeh, I knew her then. It was when you was so damn keen on getting into the army. And your Dad sent me to Sydney and that's where I met her. I kilt' a bloke over her once . . .'

'The shearers' cook.' Harry had his head in his hands. 'That was an accident.'

Jim was really crying now. 'Yeah, the shearers' cook.' He wiped his arm across his nose and pulled himself erect. 'Well, it got to me, knowing how she wouldn't help Cyn. Little black bastard she said. Look, I'm no saint. I've made jokes about Abos meself, before I met one. She's a human being, and that one treated her like dirt. Like dirt!'

Harry was unmoved.

'Jim, I don't want to hear any more. You and Cynthia have to leave. And the sooner the better.'

'Old bitch won anyway,' said Jim.

He put on his hat and took the cheque from Harry. His hands were shaking. He was thinking how he had been up in Cynthia's cottage that day. He had just packed some nighties and female stuff she wanted and was coming out the door. And he noticed Cynthia had planted some real nice pansies along the path. And then he saw the smoke and he stopped. He had put down the suitcase and was about to run for the truck, because he had always lived on the land. He knew what fire could do. And then he saw Cynthia's pansies. Her pathetic attempts along the broken bricks of her pathway to make it look pretty. And he hesitated. Because he knew it wasn't the Big House or the stables. It could have been a neighbour. No he was kidding himself. He knew what it was. And he knew whose house it was. And he thought he would give that old buzzard a damn good fright. And he thought he'd pick a bunch of pansies for Cynthia. So he sat down on the suitcase on the path and took his time. And he didn't look up until he heard the Boss's car and then he ran the truck down to the stable block to fill up the water tank. By the time he got up there, there was nothing left to save. He hadn't reckoned the fire would really kill her.

Jim came out of the office first, Liz who was watching, saw. And a long time later, Harry came out. And she got up and went in to put the kettle on to make a cup of tea for him. She never asked about Jim. He never told her. Just said they were leaving the next morning. And she had watched from her kitchen window and waited till she saw the clouds of dust in the yard that told her they were gone. And only then did she take off her apron and walk out to the garden gate and lean against it, her fingers just touching the white enamel paint of the top bar. She watched the dust until it settled. It hung over the yard for a long time. She felt more bereft at Cynthia's leaving than she had felt for any of the others.

They ate in silence on New Year's Eve until Harry said, 'I'm going for a walk.'

He pushed back his chair and went out. For a moment Liz sat listening to the quiet night and then went out after him. She caught up with him on the drive. They did not speak to each other, didn't touch each other. She began walking beside him, matching her stride to his. There was a moon which touched everything with a white light, cool but gentle. The ground was soft and dusty, fine as talcum powder under their feet. The white bark of the ghost gums loomed at them as they walked. The small bright eyes of 'possums glowed red in the dark from the highest trees. They walked to the front gate and then up a gully, past a little creek, dry now, and onto a shingled path that rose steeply. They were heading to Lookout Hill, she realized, where the electricity pylons marched across their land. Sheep and cattle pattered away from them.

As they walked Liz had a sense of them leaving things behind with each step they took. The higher they went, the more the sense of peace descended on her. She sensed that Harry felt it too. And at the top, when they finally came to a stop, the small wind, released from the confinements of the lower hills and valleys, surged around them with a new freedom. They could see the whole of Tiddalik spread before them, the vast paddocks, pale in the moonlight, that took their breath away with heat, that slammed them with cold in the winter, that broke their hearts when the rains didn't come. It was all there, all in this one patch of earth that belonged to them. And they belonged to it. It was for ever and it was better to put things behind you. Liz knew. It was the only way.

They let the wind blow them, until they felt cool and the stars above were even sharper in their brilliance. They went down the hill, their steps in harmony, their feet, familiar with the earth, not tripping over rocks or roots. Their hands brushed against each other and Liz hooked her smallest finger through his.

Tomorrow, Liz thought, she would come up here, and bring the paints Josie had given her. She would set up her canvas where she had been standing just now with Harry. She thought about it as they walked together. It would take her some weeks to get back into the rhythm again, to work out how the paints responded, how to wield the brushes, to see how the colours dried. But she would do it. Up here, where it was so beautiful, where she could see the hills, and the valleys, and the river and the house, with her paints and brushes beside her. She would try to put it all onto canvas. And she would try to paint the things she could and couldn't see; the lack of grass, the earth dormant when it should be in full flower, her love for it, and what it meant to her. And the hard things, the harsh things, she would try to paint them too. Every stump, every rock, each bone, each scar, she would paint them all. She would love them. So that they would appear, these red sheep's tracks on the hill, like fine crows'-feet around the eyes of a beloved face.